Child Law, Policy, and the School Superintendent

"Child, Law, Policy and the School Superintendent: A Handbook for New and Aspiring Chief School Administrators is mandatory reading for Chief School Administrators and Board of Education members. The practical and succinct information provided is invaluable for everyone within our great profession. I regret that I did not have access to Richard D. Tomko's insights earlier in my career. There is no question that all who ultimately are responsible for the education and welfare of students shall prosper from this gifted writer."

—**Mark J. Finkelstein**, superintendent and former president, Educational Services Commission of New Jersey; former president, New Jersey School Boards Association; former president, New Jersey Association of School Administrators

"Tomko's handbook for educational leaders is a must for aspiring as well as established superintendents. Child law and policy are subjects that confront every educational professional on a daily basis. This handbook has a place on my bookshelf right next to my copy of the department of education's administrative code. It is a new go-to text."

—**Patrick Fletcher**, superintendent of schools and former president, New Jersey Association of School Administrators

"Tomko has used his experience as a successful superintendent of schools to provide insight into those areas of administration that are not well known to aspiring chief school administrators but are extremely important to those professionals new to the office. The sections of the book that are dedicated to audits specific to the financial and governance issues in any district are vital for those administrators looking to make a seamless transition to a new district as its superintendent of schools."

—**Thomas P. Egan**, state monitor, New Jersey Department of Education; retired special agent, U.S. Department of Treasury

"All students of educational policy, school law, or school leadership should consider reading Tomko's handbook for educational leaders. There are few educational leaders in the State who have as much understanding of the practical impact that school laws and policy have on the operation of schools as Tomko. His thorough grasp of this material comes through in every chapter of the handbook, which will undoubtedly become an essential text for all aspiring educational leaders."

—**Jonathan M. Busch**, JD, MA, public school board attorney

"Not quite a textbook or a how-to manual, *Child Law, Policy, and the School Superintendent* is one of those books kept near at hand on the desk or the shelf behind the desk! Practicing superintendents will want to refresh their memory, to check something set in print. New and aspiring superintendents will want this book close at hand to have confident that their experiences are not unique to themselves. They will have a mentor-in-print as they traverse the requirements and exigencies of a new position. Tomko shares lessons learned from his own extensive and diverse experiences as a superintendent in a tone that is both collegial and helpful. He offers advice as though he was called on the phone by a colleague wanting to talk over something, or to see what he thinks. Aspiring, new, nearly-new, and experienced superintendents will all find this book to be an investment in their knowledge and competence."

—**Sister Remigia Kushner**, CSJ, director, School Leadership Program, Manhattan College

Child Law, Policy, and the School Superintendent

A Handbook for New and Aspiring Chief School Administrators

Richard D. Tomko

ROWMAN & LITTLEFIELD
Lanham • Boulder • New York • London

Published by Rowman & Littlefield
An imprint of The Rowman & Littlefield Publishing Group, Inc.
4501 Forbes Boulevard, Suite 200, Lanham, Maryland 20706
www.rowman.com

6 Tinworth Street, London SE11 5AL, United Kingdom

British Library Cataloguing in Publication Information Available

Library of Congress Cataloging-in-Publication Data

Names: Tomko, Richard D., 1973– author.
Title: Child law, policy, and the school superintendent : a handbook for new and aspiring chief school administrators / Richard D. Tomko.
Description: Lanham, Maryland : Rowman & Littlefield, [2018] | Includes bibliographical references and index.
Identifiers: LCCN 2018043055 (print) | LCCN 2018045655 (ebook) | ISBN 9781475835717 (electronic) | ISBN 9781475835694 (cloth : alk. paper) | ISBN 9781475835700 (pbk. : alk. paper)
Subjects: LCSH: School superintendents—Legal status, laws, etc.—United States. | Educational law and legislation—United States. | School management and organization—United States.
Classification: LCC KF4133 (ebook) | LCC KF4133 .T66 2018 (print) | DDC 344.73/07—dc23
LC record available at https://lccn.loc.gov/2018043055

♾️™ The paper used in this publication meets the minimum requirements of American National Standard for Information Sciences—Permanence of Paper for Printed Library Materials, ANSI/NISO Z39.48–1992.

Printed in the United States of America

For my wife, Jaimie. All of those nights she spent as a single parent to our children as I was living the pages of this handbook. There is no better teammate or partner.

Contents

Foreword   xi
Dave Hespe

Preface   xiii

Acknowledgments   xv

1   The Chief School Administrator   **1**
    What is a Superintendent or Chief School Administrator?   4
    Take a Deep Breath   5
    I.N.S.I.S.T. Protocol   6
    Perception, Law, and the Student: "Are the Buildings Safe?"   8
    New to the District?   10
    The Cabinet   11
    Certification   13
    Writing a Job Description   14
    Being Politically Savvy (Not Political)   15
    Working with the Board   15
    Utilizing the Board Attorney   16
    The Legal Opinion   17
    Utilizing an Association Attorney   18
    Liability Insurance   18
    Establishing the "Chain of Command"   19
    Know the Code of Ethics   20
    Update Trustees with Legal and Personnel Matters   21
    Diffuse a Board Meeting Issue Before it is Public   22
    Summary and Future Considerations   23

2 Education Law and Policy **25**
Board Policy 25
Affirmative Action 26
Harassment, Intimidation, and Bullying 27
Title I 29
Section 504 30
Compulsory Attendance, Truancy, and Homeschooling 32
Truancy 33
Homeschooling 35
Opting Out of Federal Assessments 38
Court-Related Case Summary: Harassment, Intimidation,
and Bullying 42
Court-Related Case Summary: Compulsory Education 42
Summary and Future Considerations 42

3 Child Welfare and Policy **45**
Confidentiality and the Rights of the Minor 45
Health Insurance Portability and Accountability Act 48
Family Educational Rights and Privacy Act 48
Supreme Court–Related Case Summary: FERPA 49
Summary and Future Considerations 50

4 Juvenile Justice Law and Policy **51**
Criminalizing School Behavior: School-to-Prison Pipeline 52
Student Threats and Preventative Discipline 54
Threats to Teachers 57
Weapons in School: Zero Tolerance 58
Students and Drugs 59
School Safety Teams 60
Student Walkouts 61
Court-Related Case Summary: First Amendment 63
Summary and Future Considerations 63

5 Family Law and Policy **65**
In *Loco Parentis v. Parens Patriae* 65
Division of Youth and Family Services (Children and
Protective Services) 66
Institutional DYFS 67
Divorce and Custody 67
McKinney-Vento Act: Homeless Children/Families 67
Summary and Future Considerations 69

6 Mental Health Law and Children **71**
Summary and Future Considerations 73

7 Children's Health Law and Policy **75**
    Life-threatening Food Allergies 75
    Immunizations 76
        Court-Related Case Summary: Immunizations 78
    Summary and Future Considerations 79

8 Resources for Child Assistance **81**
    Tragedy 81
    Mental Health Organizations 83
    Summary and Future Considerations 83

9 Writing Correspondence and Future Legal Considerations **85**
    Be Direct 85
    Be Timely 86
    Write to the Audience 86
    Be Reassuring 87
    Local Authorities, Bodies, Organizations 87
    Provide Resources (Websites) 88
    Provide Legal Research/Policies 89
    Languages 89
    Spelling/Grammar Check 89
    Attorney Review 90
    Summary and Future Considerations 90

10 "I Am Not Responsible, but I Am to Blame" **91**
    Crisis Plans 92
    Test Breaches 92
    Mandatory Professional Development 93
    Reporting Abuse 94
    National Collegiate Athletic Association Clearinghouse 94
    Cash 95
    Late Reporting (grants, etc.) 96
    Board Policy 97
    Hey, how long has that mound of soil been there? 98
    Lead and Asbestos and Mold, Oh My! 98
    Audits and Corrective Actions 99
    Protecting Students and Hiring Employees 100
    Summary and Future Considerations 101

11 How to Pass a Referendum for Construction Projects **103**
    1. Political Atmosphere 105
    2. Hiring a Consultant 105
    Parent Meetings 106
    Q & A With Legal Counsel, Bond Counsel, and Architects 106

Literature   106
3. Follow Board Policies on Electioneering   107
4. Meet With Special Interest Groups   107
5. Website   107
6. E-mail for Questions and Answers   108
7. Multiple Languages   108
8. Host Building Tours   108
Summary and Future Considerations   108

Notes   111

About the Author   117

Foreword

The superintendency has been and will remain one of the most rewarding and challenging jobs on the planet. Serving a community as the superintendent of schools will provide the opportunity for a skilled practitioner to effect change in the lives of young adults and families, as well as shape the future education policy and environment of our nation as a whole.

The superintendent wears many hats and is accountable to all stakeholders to carry out the mission of the district. He must be able to work effectively across a wide spectrum of issues, including effectively partnering with the Board of Education; developing strategies to advance the academic program; supporting stakeholders, including students, administrators, and faculty; and ensuring that there is financial stability to successfully operate the school system.

As a former school and higher education administrator and commissioner of education in New Jersey, I know firsthand the daily pressures and decisions that have to be made and the importance of working with a competent "team" to ensure that the right decisions are made in the right way with a relentless focus on what is in the best interests of children.

For a new or aspiring superintendent of schools, it is impossible to fully be aware of every problem, scenario, or mandate that one will face. A new school chief is immediately confronted with the time-consuming and important task of learning about the district and the community she serves. Although the needs of students and families are different in every district in every state across the country, there are certain successful practices, policies, protocols, and regulatory compliance issues that each new chief school administrator should be familiar with as they walk into office that first day in September.

This handbook was developed for new and aspiring chief school administrators to help them survive the initial learning curve and then thrive as an educational leader. What Richard Tomko provides to the student and reader in these chapters is an outline of those potential issues that a school superintendent will face involving such things as education law and policy, mental health for students, student and teacher safety, the political atmosphere of the "office," and working together with the board of education. Using his considerable experiences and successes in district leadership positions as a bridge, Tomko identifies for aspiring colleagues those pertinent areas of practice, policy, and law that affect the daily operations of the central office and that will ultimately make the difference in the success of the district.

—Dave Hespe
New Jersey Commissioner of Education,
1999–2001, 2014–2016

Preface

This handbook has been designed as a tool to be utilized by administrators currently in the field, those new and seasoned administrators who may be beginning their first year as a chief school administrator, board of education trustees looking to examine the role of the school superintendent as chief school administrator, and those graduate students in educational leadership courses who are working within lectures to bridge the theory with practice as they prepare for leadership roles and standardized licensing exams that require a formidable knowledge of the world of the school superintendent.

As a proponent of having a strong knowledge base as it pertains to the broad scope of the core principles of child law and administrative policies in dealing with the day-to-day interactions of the "office," each chapter provides the reader with insight into an integral process pertinent to a topic paramount to the success of any leader who has been elevated, or aspires as such, to the role of school's chief in any district in the United States. Though specific laws and protocols may be attenuated across borders, the basic concepts, theories, and obstacles remain the same.

There is no one—or twenty books—that can define and prepare a school administrator for every situation that he will face on any given day. However, there are specific areas of the job description that can be learned and used as a foundation for further investigation and inquiry into particular decisions and matters of interest. A true leader can never be too prepared for any mission, especially when she is charged with strengthening the future of the community and encouraging fortitude in her administrators, teachers, and students.

This is not a law book. Rather, this is a journey into some of the common areas of the school superintendency and insight into how specific issues should be recognized by lead administrators within a school system. The concepts outlined within these chapters are there to help individuals prepare for an administrative promotion to chief school administrator, as well as identify the most common situations a new or aspiring superintendent may face during his first year in office. As always, any superintendent or building or district administrator should look to consult with his board attorney for legal advice specific to each incident prior to making any decisions that will affect students and personnel or cause action to be taken based on specific state laws and local policies.

Acknowledgments

I would like to acknowledge Maureen Kieffer, JD, and Kathleen Hirsman, JD, professors at Loyola University Chicago School of Law, for assisting me in authoring such a handbook by guiding me through the concepts within its chapters.

Chapter 1

The Chief School Administrator

The Buck Stops Here!

—Harry S. Truman

It's 3:04 on a Friday afternoon, and you just finished a memorandum to the board trustees discussing some changes you will be recommending to the substance abuse policy for first reading at the board meeting next week. The weekend promises some relaxation from the district, with plans to visit relatives and enjoy watching your son's baseball game against high school rival Vanderbilt on Saturday afternoon. Just then, you receive a call on your cellphone from your high school principal.

"Hey, Steve. What's up?"

Your administrator responds with some urgency, "Doc, you have a minute? I think we may have a problem over here."

As the most "seasoned" member of your team, Steve goes on to explain that a teacher approached him that afternoon to report a disturbing "rumor" that she overheard from students who were congregating in the hallway outside her classroom. You quickly learn that several female students had received gifts of jewelry from a young male teacher a few weeks earlier. After hearing the report, the principal did some further investigating, which led to him uncovering other allegations that now question the welfare of several students in his building.

This is a real scenario of what comes across your desk as a chief school administrator (CSA). What happens next in the scenario is you acting to ensure that your students are safe, the board and district are protected, and you uphold the law and board policy in a consistent manner. What happens next in the scenario also has implications of your role as a leader and your ability to manage a district effectively. Each step you make throughout

1

the process can and will be scrutinized for accuracy, fairness, and a legal standing.

You will be critiqued along the way and assessed based on your effectiveness in both handling the situation and the ultimate outcomes from your decisions. Regardless of the end result, the process you use to determine what "tools" you will utilize as a vehicle toward making these decisions is the most important consideration in your leadership role. Although the process includes a scientific method of observing, recording data, and making educated assumptions when reaching these conclusions, one can argue that your knowledge of law as it relates to children and the educational system posts high on the hierarchy of needs for an established CSA, working on an issue or a crisis at hand.

Referencing the theories and tenets surrounding the field of child law has become a daily necessity for the success and survival of every district superintendent of schools. The office of the CSA includes daily challenges relevant to the success of a school district, including ensuring the continuity of educational instruction relevant to the curriculum; following policies and procedures that are governed by central office mandates and directives; and protecting the overall safety and wellness of the students, faculty, and staff who come to the district each and every day to live the established mission.

In fact, the seat of the superintendent is filled with constantly changing problems and decisions that have to be made, which will ultimately support one faction of constituents and isolate the other. Regardless, with each new day comes a new decision to be made that will affect the lives of students, staff members, local government, families, and the community at large. Therefore, it is important in your role as the superintendent of schools to be consistent with your decisions and, most important, ensure that you are making these decisions based on research, educational policy, and the law.

Just as a superintendent is familiar with the daily routines, strengths, and weaknesses of his principals and administrators, a seasoned superintendent also knows his own strengths and weaknesses in dealing with the political implications surrounding the "office." He can identify the hot topic items that can bring attention to his district in less than a moment's notice and the matters surrounding educational leadership, management, and policy that fill his desktop.

Where one district leader's strength may be curriculum, another individual may thrive in the area of organizational structure, crisis management, or finance. A seasoned superintendent admits that although he may be fluent in every area that necessitates the role, he must surround himself with a leadership team that enlists true leaders with strengths that complement the superintendent's weaknesses. This is why most central office teams include an assistant superintendent, personnel or human resource director, a business administrator, curriculum director, athletic supervisor, and other independent department heads to help direct the flow of the needs of the district.

Although the superintendent can always look to his "team" for guidance in making decisions and assistance in providing a positive educational environment for students, faculty, and staff, there is one area pertaining to his most important constituents—the children in district—where he must be well versed in order to protect the district, board trustees, faculty, and himself when making important decisions. This area is child law, specifically the areas of education law; child welfare law; and the maintenance of important legal practices, protocols, and procedures that are imperative to the successful function of the superintendent.

The theories, case studies, and laws outlined in this handbook are meant to provide the superintendent with a cursory knowledge of specific legal issues and situations most likely to arise and that are most important. This handbook is in no way meant to dissuade the reader from discussing each situation with a board attorney; rather, it is a guide to help familiarize oneself with what actions can be taken and precedents that have been used in similar instances.

Barring politics and relationships with your board, there are only several major categories of events that can occur where you may possibly find yourself in a compromised position, causing your approval rating to plummet and/ or threatening your job security. The first of these categories is job performance. In the field of education, there are constant and inconsistent "checks and balances" put in place that rank proficiency ratings in nearly every area of student and teacher performance.

These include, but are not limited to, scores on assessments, graduation rates, chronic absenteeism, suspension/expulsion percentages, student growth percentiles, SAT scores, and college and career readiness markers. As you establish goals for both yourself and your board, reaching and even surpassing certain expected levels of proficiency in one or several of these areas is a necessary factor in gauging a CSA's success and longevity in district.

The second category impacting the position is policy. As a board's sole responsibility is to establish policies to ensure the appropriate function and direction of a district, it is the superintendent's main purpose to ensure that the policies are followed accordingly. A superintendent who disagrees with a policy and how it effects the educational environment must work with her board to change said policy and its regulation to advance the educational mission forward. Absent of that change, established policies stand out as the outline for the day-to-day operations of the district, contracted personnel, and students.

Thus, a superintendent who chooses not to follow policy finds himself governing his district against what has been established by the board. One must remember that the board is representative of different factions of a community and was elected (or appointed) to represent these factions in the decision-making process.

In return for community and constituent support, there is an expectation of board trustees to work to provide a quality education for the youth of the community and, in turn, create an educational awareness that establishes a sense of prowess and pride in how that community compares to others in neighboring regions, the same state, and similar demographic standards.

The final category that can impact decisions and performance is legal issues that the district and administration may face in consideration of child law and the processes surrounding the everyday mission of the district. In most cases when dealing with minors and school-aged children, there are specific instances where understanding the laws governing the field and protections/rights of children, employees, and parents are critical in beginning the process of reviewing policies, establishing school site or systematic protocols, or discussing issues with members of your team and others.

Granted, the superintendent has a board attorney who is available for consultation; however, each situation that may have a legal basis or a necessity of cause based on a legal implication must first be identified by you in order to request even something as simple as an attorney opinion or review. It is important to be able to have some reference in consideration of common legal issues that include children and school districts in this ever-changing society.

WHAT IS A SUPERINTENDENT OR CHIEF SCHOOL ADMINISTRATOR?

Throughout the handbook, the terms *superintendent* and *chief school administrator* appear and can be used interchangeably in every instance. As districts include specific title names based on past practice, region of the country, licensing pertinent to state requirements, or other reason set forth, at the end of the day the chief education officer (CEO) of each and every school district in the nation has the ultimate responsibility of all district decisions and operations in consideration of the operation of the district schools, programs, fiscal management, students, faculty, and staff.

A superintendent or CSA is a licensed supervisor whose mission is to inspire and lead every member of his administrative and instructional team in establishing and achieving the mission and standards of excellence as established by the local board of education trustees. The superintendent or CSA works with his board to establish policies and procedures to guide and manage the schools in accordance with federal and state laws, as well as administrative code.

TAKE A DEEP BREATH

There aren't too many decisions made while wearing the CSA's hat that must be made immediately. Rather, a superintendent will always need to react to all situations by providing some type of "answer" at the time the situation arises. These answers and responses should include both specific and general statements so that each individual asking the question (whether it be a board member, teacher, administrator, parent, or a member of the community) is assured by the superintendent's statements that he understands what it is that is being asked of him and that the superintendent may need to do more research so that he may provide a more informed answer.

Not giving an immediate answer is not a sign of weakness. Instead, a deliberate pause protects not only the superintendent but the board and district as well. This is a common mistake made by "rookie" administrators who answer questions at board and public meetings where a member of the public demands an answer, and the answer given by the administrator comes back to "haunt" him months or even years later. With social media being prevalent in today's society as it is and the ability to create and maintain public records for an infinite period of time, a quick and unresearched answer can follow you and your career for a long time to follow.

This strategy does not suggest that certain questions couldn't be answered. There are definite matters relevant to the educational process in the district that can be answered on the spot, including, but not limited to, dates and times of events, descriptions of programs, textbook titles, sport team records, and the like where the audience is made to feel confident that its superintendent has the pulse of the district and community in her best interest.

On the other hand, if information is asked of the superintendent, and she is not absolutely sure of an answer or it is a question or comment that calls for her to do more research, then it is imperative that she acknowledges the question and ends with a clear "I will need to follow up with you when I have more information for you." The superintendent must always utilize her position at the top of the administrative hierarchy and use the district team to ensure the promotion of a transparent atmosphere that provides correct information and direct responses to questions asked of the superintendent of schools.

Utilizing legal opinions and state statutes, student data, and attorney input and referencing board policies in responses made to specific questions provide a safe and solid foundation on which a superintendent will base her decisions. If the superintendent provides an answer without those types of backup references, then her decisions seem based only on opinion and are not data driven.

As the CSA position is most removed from building leadership positions that may include daily decisions that need to be made immediately, superintendents have the ability to utilize any and all resources to command the most appropriate decision for the situation at hand. Most important, as district constituents know this to be the case, there is a strong expectation that the answer will be best suited for the district and the "right answer."

I.N.S.I.S.T. PROTOCOL

With each passing incident, a successful CSA processes a series of directional leadership "steps" in order to be comfortable with the decisions being made with regard to the incident with which he is faced. Throughout an administrative career, administrators tend to formulate this decision-making system from what was learned from those leaders they had worked "for" in the same or similar leadership roles.

Although modeling after an individual's leadership style is effective, every successful educational leader learns more by dissecting the "mistakes" made by those same leaders. Hence, over the years, working with/under the different personalities and leadership styles of those individuals in both district and school leadership roles provides a CSA with a toolbox of procedures that she may use to bring success to her district during her tenure.

The study of administration reveals one ultimate thing—every school and every district is different. That statement isn't meant to exist as some epiphanic moment in time that "knocks a newbie off of his chair" as he reads it. Rather, it becomes the quintessential mantra in consideration of understanding that what works in one district just doesn't work in another. Therefore, there will come a time when a superintendent's proverbial toolbox full of the procedures and protocols he has learned from the rights and wrongs of his leader-idols becomes rusted shut.

Over time, a superintendent will continuously add, review, and attenuate those "go-to" methods that she will use to give direction and solve for situations. But regardless of how many of those protocols and methods change throughout her tenure in a current, past, or future district, the process that the CSA utilizes each and every day for nearly every situation must follow a specific protocol to help answer and respond to every situation.

The I.N.S.I.S.T. Protocol (Figure 1.1) design ensures that the CSA and members of the administrative cabinet have an effective measure of checks and balances by assuring that a crisis or issue at hand is vetted when considering all areas pertinent to the students and district in conjunction with law, policy, and the appropriate protocols to follow and then act on when a crisis occurs. Most often, the original problem that arises is not what becomes the

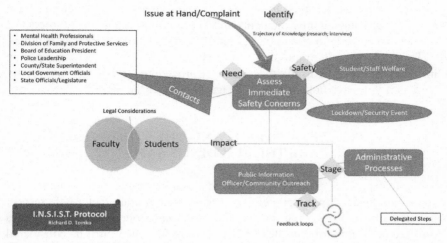

Figure 1.1   I.N.S.I.S.T. Protocol

main problem. In other words, superintendents and their administrators, who do not deal with the intricacies of all possible outcomes in consideration of a crisis, most often become victims of "educational shrapnel," in that a basic fix to a problem becomes more complex due to outliers.

The six major components, as outlined by the acronym, include:

- Identify: (What is the issue/problem/imminent threat?)
- Need: needs assessment (Who, what, where, when?)
- Safety: (Are students, faculty, community/facilities safe from danger?)
- Impact: (What is the potential impact and outcome from the problem?)
- Stage: execute plan and processes
- Track: follow the outcomes and prepare for follow-up (feedback loops)

As observed in the protocol figure, the impact on students and faculty in any situation includes possible legal ramifications that must be considered with each and every incident. Without considering both the individual laws and statutes that were affected as well as those laws and statutes that must be followed (e.g., reporting guidelines for incidents, approvals, audits) after an issue or incident is discovered leaves both the superintendent and the district susceptible to lawsuits; prolongs the situation at hand; and, frankly, can become a professional embarrassment.

Unless a practicing lawyer, the superintendent cannot be expected to know and opine on every aspect of education, labor, and employment law for which he may come in contact with during the daily operations of the district. However, he must have an ability to identify the impact and legal ramifications surrounding incidents and, more important, the legal impact of the decisions made in attempting to rectify those identified crisis situations.

Thus, it is virtually impossible to state that the superintendent has made an informed decision as to the delegation of procedures to react to and rectify a crisis if you have not assessed the legal impact of the identified problems.

PERCEPTION, LAW, AND THE STUDENT: "ARE THE BUILDINGS SAFE?"

The art of positive perception is one of the most important phenomena of successful leadership. If "perception" wasn't an important factor with respect to our daily routines, then we wouldn't landscape our lawns! Providing a positive perception of the role of CSA is an art form that must be considered from the first meet-and-greet until the final day in district. Perception plays a key role in the success of any leader in every organization. When considering the role of CSA, there are several integral and important issues that affect the outcome of performance, district advancement, and achievement levels in which the superintendent will be ultimately evaluated for with regard to the confidence a community and its board will place in the superintendent and his tenure in the position.

The community wants a leader who can boost scores and graduation rates to enhance real estate values and township rankings while keeping the tax base low and spending to a minimum. The superintendent's credentials, past administrative experience, and expertise in an area important to the vision of the district are just a few of the reasons why the superintendent is perceived to be that leader to move the district forward. With all of this, it is overly important to be as prepared as possible for any and all situations that can arise where one can delegate members of the leadership team to assist him in handling an issue prior to it "spiraling" out of control.

In this role, the CSA needs to be confident that what is in place works and what doesn't can and will be fixed. As parents, we leave our children in the authority of school personnel for approximately 12 percent of any given year with the expectation that they will master the skills needed to be successful in the twenty-first-century global workplace, eat a balanced meal (or two), enhance their academic aptitude in core subject areas, and excel in extracurricular activities to promote a competitive spirit and strengthen social skills.

Superintendents are aware that the greatest commodity is the students and their safety is the top priority. Understanding the legal basis for all decisions and actions; the requirements from federal, state, and local authoritative bodies; and the plans of action to ensure that the correct protocols are established and followed through is critical to a superintendent's success in district.

As it is impossible to know all of the established practices and appropriate procedures to follow in consideration of policies, law, and the like when first elevated to the position, researching issues, asking for assistance, and making informed, consistent decisions will permit the superintendent to continue to grow in the field and retain the knowledge set needed that acts as the true foundation for the job at hand and the daily challenges faced in this key administrative role.

It is important when addressing colleagues, parents, or community groups to maintain control within any given situation and answer questions truthfully with research and/or data to support statements. Perception of an ability to lead is a key factor when garnering positive approval from stakeholders and fostering a strong relationship between the CSA and school board.

An example of this is that of a "seasoned" superintendent of schools who is presenting the board and the community with their strategic plan where he lists ten goals to enhance the academic environment of the district schools. He commands the room exuding such eloquence and confidence that everyone believes that these goals would each be met by June of the following year. It isn't for his lack of trying, but ten goals are a large number to manage where resources can become limited due to an attenuated concentration in specific areas of the school system as a whole.

Regardless, the "drive," excitement, faculty "buy-in," and overall momentum that was perceived from that opening meeting helped create a contagious, positive climate that proved that the superintendent was a true transformational leader with a vision and supporting plan for the district. Being confident when making decisions based on one's knowledge of a situation and the parameters that must be followed in consideration of policy, law, fiduciary barriers, and the needs of students and personnel (no matter how little or how great amount of knowledge one may have in consideration of a situation) allows others to be confident in the superintendent's ability to assume the position and urges all to become an integral part of the team as well.

The diagram[1] shows the basic "Daily Educational Environment" that a CSA must navigate through on an everyday basis in order to ensure the smooth and responsible transition of the district, one workday to the next. Each day, responsibilities are broken down into four (4) major quadrants where outcomes for issues within each quadrant can affect the overall success of the district or school system at any given time. These quadrants are: Institutional Policies and Politics; Stakeholder Input and Community Participation; Curriculum, Programs, Testing Assessments, and Procedures; and The Institutional Culture (see figure 1.2).

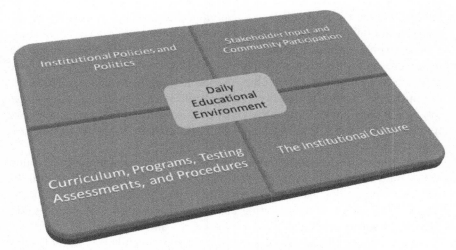

Figure 1.2   Daily Educational Environment of a Chief School Administrator

NEW TO THE DISTRICT?

As a newly appointed superintendent "settles" into the position, he is faced with a long list of programmatic initiatives, constituent and stakeholder concerns, and learning the political landscape of the community. Although there are a multitude of tasks to consider, the most important first step is to establish baseline data with regard to infrastructure, academic goals, and the status of district finances. Think of a police chief stepping into her headquarters the first day on the job.

Although there may be a plethora of problems to list on the docket for her new position, her initial point of business is to inventory the evidence "locker." This is an important benchmark in consideration of what the new chief has "inherited" or not inherited from the previous administration. In other words, six months after being elevated to her new position and someone is looking for evidence that is now missing, if there was an inventory taken on day 1 and that evidence is not listed there, then the new chief isn't to blame.

The same holds very true for a new superintendent and what he has inherited from the previous lead administrator. Over the course of the first ninety days, part of the entry plan must include desktop, formal, and/or informal audits of many of the systems that are in place in district. This procedure is important for two major reasons.

First, just like the new police chief, the superintendent now has baseline data to fully understand the immediate needs and considerations with regard to specific compliance issues and federal and state statutory regulations. This type of auditing includes, but is not limited to, teacher certification, fingerprinting for employees/background checks, comprehensive annual financial reports (CAFRs), cash flow balances, transportation safety logs, Federal Title funds, and so on.

Lastly, audits of this nature will assist a new CSA in understanding lapses in systems that may need immediate remediation. For example, an audit of fingerprints leads to the realization that none of the paraprofessionals hired in the past seven years have been fingerprinted. An immediate action plan must include a certification process for those individuals and an assurance that all appropriate documentation will be received by a specified time period. Remember, the safety of the students is the top priority of the CSA in any district, and these types of compliance issues are extremely important in consideration of meeting that mission.

THE CABINET

There is much research in the field to define what leadership styles and individual tendencies a CSA seeks in defining the administrative council or cabinet. One can argue the different characteristics that should be innate within a particular building-level or district administrator in order to ensure a smooth transition and make a strong impact on a new agenda to lead the schools. A good CSA immediately understands that he has inherited the majority of his administrative team and with the exception of a few different officers who may be new, the current positions are "entrenched" in the previous way of operating the district.

This isn't always a "bad" thing, and the first rule when entering a new district is to observe all operations before making changes (unless immediate changes are necessary for compliance and/or legal issues). With that being said, the quicker one learns the strengths and weaknesses of his core team members, the quicker he will find himself making greater progress in district. This may lead to reauthoring job descriptions, creating new titles, and even transferring individuals to different, more suitable positions.

This should be seen as an opportunity to move the district forward by designing a new hierarchical chart and organizational structure. In consideration of structuring a desired council or cabinet to assist a new CSA in

Table 1.1 Cabinet Positions and Responsibilities

	Supervisory Responsibilities	Student Governance	Personnel	Fiscal Regulatory Responsibilities	Federal Title Monies	Child Welfare
Assistant/Deputy Superintendent	✓	✓	✓	✓	✓	✓
Assistant Superintendent for Curriculum and Instruction	✓	✓	✓	✓	✓	✓
Business Administrator	✓		✓	✓	✓	✓
Public Information Officer		✓				✓
Director of Operations	✓	✓	✓	✓	✓	✓
Director of Research, Data, and Planning		✓		✓	✓	✓
Director of Testing		✓	✓		✓	✓
Director of Special Services	✓	✓	✓	✓	✓	✓
Director of Pupil Personnel Services	✓	✓	✓		✓	✓
Director of Safety Services	✓	✓	✓			✓
Director of Human Resources		✓	✓			✓
Chief Innovation Officer		✓		✓	✓	✓
Chief Talent Officer		✓	✓	✓	✓	✓
Chief Partnership Officer		✓			✓	✓
Compliance Officer		✓	✓	✓		✓

ensuring both growth and statutory compliance issues, the following positions should be considered (see table 1.1).

CERTIFICATION

Every state requires an educator preparation program that leads to a certification in order for specific individuals to attain employment and remain in good standing in the public school sector. Although many individuals graduate and enter the "traditional" teaching route, almost every state offer alternates routes for teacher and administrator certification for professionals who may be entering education as a second career or did not graduate with a degree in the education field.

In Texas, for example, teacher certification requires candidates to complete a state-approved teacher certification program and hold at least a bachelor's degree. To earn standard certification, candidates must complete educational requirements (coursework), pass certification exams, and fulfill a criminal history/background check.

In a state like New Jersey, teacher applicants must hold a bachelor's degree, complete an approved teacher preparation program, and pass the required standard examinations for specific teaching areas. This is considered a traditional route to state certification, and it leads to a Certificate of Eligibility with Advanced Standing (CEAS) endorsement, which allows a prospective candidate to seek employment. Once that individual has a promise of employment by a school district, the candidate receives a provisional teaching license, which leads to standard certification after the completion of a mentoring process.

In other states like New York and Alaska, after a bachelor's degree is earned, certification exams passed to proficiency, and a teacher preparation program is verified, licensure is issued in a "tiered" system where an initial certificate is upgraded to a professional certification after several years of successful teaching, professional development hours, and/or an appropriate master's degree.

It is imperative that the CSA, her direct confidential executive assistant, and the director/manager of human resources fully understand the road map to certification in their state and the credentials that each and every individual needs to teach or supervise a specific course, department, grade level, and the like throughout the entire district.

The importance of assuring that an individual teacher's certification matches the subject area or discipline that he has been assigned cannot be stressed enough. Further, it is imperative that those in charge of checking the credentials receive professional development and legal updates as changes to these regulations come very frequently. It is also important to note that just because a résumé states that someone graduated with a degree or completed a preparation program, it doesn't necessarily certify that it has occurred.

Your human resource assistant must check the official transcript of every employee to verify graduation date, degree obtained, and credits earned for salary and certification purposes and cross-reference this information with what was provided by the candidate on his résumé and application.

WRITING A JOB DESCRIPTION

Even though job descriptions are not "legal" documents, they can define parameters that may be useful in consideration of evaluating the specific job performance of employees, making the description an important tool when faced with the difficult task of terminating an individual's employment in case performance issues become apparent. Accurate job descriptions provide a basis for job evaluation and salary structure and protect the district's interests by enabling the board and administration to produce documentation of an employee's duties.

A job description should list areas to verify competency (e.g., application and résumé criteria, academic competency, credentials, limitations) and terms of employment (e.g., length of work-year, salary, conditions established by law, and policies of the board of education). Descriptions should also include qualifications required to be in compliance with federal labor law, certification(s) needed for the position, physical and environmental demands placed on the employee in the position, and other qualifications mandated by the CSA and the local education agency. These may include the following:

- Proof of U.S. citizenship or legal resident alien status (federal Form I-9 in compliance with the Immigration Reform and Control Act of 1986).
- Criminal record history check with clearance given by the state's department of education.
- Health record and examination is adequate to fulfill the job functions and responsibilities with reasonable accommodation pursuant to 42 U.S.C. 12101 and in accordance with federal and state statutes.
- Physical demands that must be met by an employee to successfully perform the essential responsibilities and functions of the job including:

  a. lifting items;
  b. sitting, standing, and walking for required periods of time;
  c. using close vision, color vision, peripheral vision, and depth perception, along with the ability to focus vision;
  d. communicating effectively in English, using proper grammar and vocabulary;
  e. reaching with hands and arms and using hands and fingers to handle objects and operate tools, computers, and/or controls;

f. exposure to a variety of childhood and adult diseases and illnesses;

g. occasional exposure to a variety of weather conditions;

h. exposure to heated/air and ventilated facilities;

i. exposure to a building in which a variety of chemical substances are used for cleaning, instruction, and/or operation of equipment; and

j. functioning in a workplace that is usually moderately quiet but that can be noisy at times (specifically for building positions).

Finally, a job description should always conclude with a caveat that states, "Perform all other assignments/duties or that may be required by the superintendent of schools (chief school administrator) or his/her designee."

BEING POLITICALLY SAVVY (NOT POLITICAL)

It is important in consideration of legal, ethical, and moral standards that the tenure of the CSA is not marred with allegations that his office is a political podium for personal gain. Let's face it—politics plays some part of the "job"; however, it is important to refrain from becoming political and remain being politically savvy. Crossing into the political world of the school superintendency will bring with the journey a plethora of highs and lows, meaning that a "political" CSA will be in and out of favor each time the pendulum swings to one "side" or the other.

In addition, political favors, pressure, or decisions based on political influence can cause ethical complaints to be filed and other legal ramifications. In today's world of social media, even a nonguilty verdict can be overshadowed by a lead story placed on an information blog or other website that can be captured each and every time someone googles a name. Rather, being aware of the important players involved, in each and every situation, is a more productive way to influence matters and remove oneself from any connections and/or implications.

Remember, the tide ebbs and flows when considering all matters of a school district and the political environment within. A CSA must not become part of a board member's political agenda but rather know what that agenda is and how to work within and around it.

WORKING WITH THE BOARD

"You always get your say, but you don't always get your way!" As a "young" administrator, this advice sometimes seems to go in one ear and out the other. As time moved on and experience settles in, one slowly comes to understand that in this profession, there are many opinions and agendas that seem to intertwine with professional recommendations that, at times, interfere with the progress expected of the CSA.

It is important to recognize the board as a true representation of the community that it collectively serves. Each and every day is successful if the CSA can leave her office saying to herself, "Everyone is safe, all policies were upheld, and I made each and every decision in a consistent manner based on research, legal parameters, and above all what is best for my students in the district." Working with the board is the most important dynamic to consider in the job, and how successful a CSA is in this manner will ultimately cast how successful she will be in moving the mission of her administration and the district forward.

As a team, the superintendent and board create policies to enhance the school environment and ensure that the district is in compliance in all matters of governance, finance, personnel, instruction, and program. It is equally important that the board trustees firmly know that the superintendent has their "best" interests in mind and will be providing them guidance and legal standing for recommendations and referrals. The more transparent the superintendent is in each process followed to reach a specific decision to make certain recommendations, the easier it is for trustees to support a recommendation as it is based on evidence and research.

UTILIZING THE BOARD ATTORNEY

With respect to the law and education policy, the board attorney chosen by the trustees is obviously the most formidable ally when dealing with the day-to-day issues involving the district, students, and school personnel. This is arguably the most important relationship to foster in district right alongside that of the Board president and trustees.

As certain decisions made will necessitate a call or conference with the board attorney, it is imperative that a trusting relationship continues to grow to ensure that the superintendent and attorney are working in tandem to move the district forward. In consideration of this relationship, there is one key factor that a successful CSA must remember in his dealings with the board attorney. Simply put, this is the board's attorney.

As the relationship will undoubtedly lead to many great accomplishments for the district, the attorney's main duty is to protect the board, and although the CSA is considered a nonvoting member of that "team," there will come a time when the CSA is questioned about something or is negotiating the contract and the true boundaries of the relationship will be drawn. Regardless, the board attorney is the greatest resource when attempting to change a policy, deliver a reprimand, or in the face of possible future litigation based on a decision made or a recommendation put forth for board approval.

Further, it is always better to have the support of the attorney when making recommendations for formal board approval, in case legal questions do arise during and after the resolution is approved. In consideration of the different areas of legal matters that may arise throughout the district, several different attorneys should be utilized who have specialties in a specific area of law to fulfill the needs of the community. Some examples include:

- special education,
- bond counsel (referendum projects, leasing),
- policy, and
- contract negotiations/labor law.

Hence, it is important to consider what is known as a "full-service" law firm, which has partners and other legal personnel to handle any and all legal considerations. That's not to say that a local, single-attorney firm does not have the aptitude to handle your legal needs; rather, it is sometimes easier, especially in larger districts, to have all litigation matters organized and defended by members of the same team familiar with all aspects of the district.

THE LEGAL OPINION

Arguably, one of the most important resources that your attorney can provide is the formal legal opinion. Although, as CSA, all the responsibility rests on your shoulders, being able to follow a legal opinion on the record can prove to be an extremely important asset when faced with the responsibility of defending a decision you made that comes back to "haunt you." If you are questioned by members of the board, an arbitrator, or judge, the legal opinion can be used to provide a legal basis as to why you made a particular decision or acted on a situation in a specific manner.

A good legal opinion includes state statute as well as researched case law that supports the opinion. The opinion most likely will not suggest a course of action for a situation that arises for which you called for the opinion. The decision itself is your job. The opinion should give you the information necessary to make an informed decision.

UTILIZING AN ASSOCIATION ATTORNEY

Most superintendents/CSAs belong to a national, state, and/or local association (Union). Many contracts for CSAs include the costs associated with such entities within the scope of the contract. Besides networking, professional literature, and professional development opportunities, there will come a time when a superintendent will need the assistance of an attorney to represent her with regard to negotiations, decisions made, and even disagreements with board members.

Although the superintendent sits as a nonvoting member of the board and will utilize the board's (district) attorney on a daily basis for the operational component of the job, the board attorney ultimately represents the board and district in all aspects of the district. Hence, when the "going gets rough," there is no gray area when the board attorney needs to decide which "side" to take—the board always wins.

It is important that an association attorney is kept apprised of any and all situations occurring in district or between the superintendent and a member of the board in a timely manner. Most often, CSAs reach out to their association attorneys as a reaction to something that has occurred. As is one of the underlying theses of this handbook, the successful school leader is more proactive than reactive.

Transformative school administrators have been known (on one occasion or two) to be those leaders who do what they know is right for the students and the district, knowing that it may not be a popular decision in the community. Having said this, superintendents have been known not to ask advice as to whether or not something is ethically, legally, and morally "right," but moreover the question, "How much trouble can I get into when I do this?" CSAs must take serious caution in taking that point of view when navigating a district through both calm and tumultuous "waters."

However, it is wholly important—or rather essential—that a CSA is comfortable with his association attorney and her ability to understand the way he leads and his passion for the job. A superintendent may be more comfortable with someone who is conservative on issues or he may be looking for a legal companion who understands that making a difference sometimes means that one must go against the status quo and speak up for his students and his district. Most important, he must have confidence in and be comfortable with whom he chooses to represent him.

LIABILITY INSURANCE

In the scope of the job description and daily routines of the office, the board must indemnify a CSA from any legal actions or suits brought against her and the board, as she is acting in the capacity of the due performance of her office. A CSA should assure that such a clause exists in her contract in order to protect her from any legality or claims that may arise during her tenure. Such a clause may read as follows:

> *Professional Liability*. The board agrees that it shall defend, hold harmless, and indemnify the superintendent/chief school administrator from any and all demands, claims, suits, actions, and legal proceedings brought against the superintendent/CSA in his individual capacity or in his official capacity as agent and/or employee of the board, provided the incident, which is the subject of any such demand, claim, suit, action or legal proceeding, arose while the superintendent/CSA was acting within the scope of his employment (Model Contract Language). If, in the good faith opinion of the superintendent/CSA, a conflict exists in regard to the defense of any claim, demand or action brought against him, and the position of the board in relation thereto, the superintendent/CSA may engage his own legal counsel, in which event the board shall indemnify the superintendent/CSA for the costs of his legal defense. The board further agrees to cover the superintendent/CSA under the board's liability insurance policies, including employment practices liability coverage, in the minimum amount of $___ million.

It is also suggested that an administrator carry additional insurance under an "umbrella" within a homeowner's policy to protect him from any professional liability that may come in question with regard to said liability falling within the scope of the performance of his duties. This may include something that was said outside of the workday but at a school function that may potentially harm someone or a suit with which the superintendent is served that claims he acted in an egregious manner and where the board, on the onset of the claim, refuses to indemnify him for the action. Such a section of the policy should relate to "Personal Injury," with subsection offenses occurring during the policy term as (1) "Libel," (2) "Slander," and (3) "Defamation of Character."

ESTABLISHING THE "CHAIN OF COMMAND"

As due process is important to any systematic norm in relation to solving for a problem or incident, the same holds true in consideration of the chain of command. In dealing with situations with students and personnel, it is imperative that a policy be structured with regard to the chain in such a way as to provide for a smooth transition from one office or department to the next in an attempt to mitigate any concern that may lead to a potential issue for the district. Further, being consistent by assuring that the chain of command is followed in nearly every situation forces a work environment in which one will not engage on a path to micromanaging.

Having stakeholders follow the chain of command, as it is backed by a formalized board policy and published to parents in handbooks and via website portals, also allows principals and other members of the administrative team the ability to manage their buildings or department effectively, permitting them to make compromises with their parent base and portray the claim that they can handle their problem by having an appropriate conversation and weighing in all possible outcomes.

Although there are many different situations to consider, the foundation for the proverbial "chain of command" when dealing with student issues always begins with the classroom teacher. Any policy, meeting, or communication protocols should identify that questions and concerns with students must first include a discussion between the classroom teacher and that student's parent or guardian. If that discussion occurs and the parent or guardian still does not agree with the outcome and wishes to discuss the situation further, the next "link" in the chain would include the building principal.

After the building principal works to mitigate any concerns and the parent or guardian still does not feel that the outcome is appropriate, then a member of the central office or district administration would be the next official to discuss the concerns with the student and parent. After all of those means are exhausted, the final part of the chain leads to the office of the superintendent. It is important to stress that this is not a deflection of an issue that is happening in district. Rather, the chain preserves a consistent means of allowing the appropriate, building-level personnel, most directly related to the issue, the ability to act on and attempt to solve all issues in a collaborative manner. Indeed, some issues do call for the superintendent to become immediately involved. These would include complaints with regard to the welfare of students, the integrity of the office, and/or matters that consider board members and the cabinet.

KNOW THE CODE OF ETHICS

The code of ethics sets clear expectations and guiding practice to inspire professional excellence in the field of education. Professional educators believe that a common set of principles helps individuals gauge professional judgment when making decisions that affect students, teachers, and other components of a school system. An infringement of this code can lead to censure, suspension, and even termination, not always by a direct initiation but public opinion as well.

Each state has its own code of ethics that establishes the rule of general conduct for all educators, administrators, and board members in a district, with some states having a more in-depth and formal code than others.

Although the tenets of this code seem to emulate basic concepts of a true understanding of the education profession and working with students, there are some specific parts of the code that one must demonstrate an awareness of so as to not get entangled with unnecessary legal considerations when defending yourself from an alleged "ethics" charge. Although most of what is outlined within a state's individual ethics act is not of a pure legal matter, the legal implications come into force when an administrator is attempting to explain what had occurred or justifying his actions.

Using the code as a moral compass when making decisions allows a superintendent to navigate the situation at hand more efficiently. Should someone question her decision, she could always use the code as one of the basic guides followed in the decision-making process. Regardless, knowing the code prior to the first day in office is imperative to molding a leadership style indicative of the tone and manner a superintendent should use when moving the district forward.

UPDATE TRUSTEES WITH LEGAL AND PERSONNEL MATTERS

The superintendent's responsibility to the district, students, community, and faculty includes a myriad of "bullets" starting with safety and academic program and ending with test scores and assessments. The CSA's responsibility to the board, however, is much simpler—keep the trustees informed of all happenings and shield them from being embarrassed. Obviously, the job entails a "bit" more than that, but a major evaluative measure includes how the superintendent works with his board in maintaining a strict line of communication with them that includes the critical issues and daily happenings around district.

When it comes to legal matters and issues with personnel, it is important to keep the trustees abreast of all situations; however, the CSA must use caution when reporting specific legal concerns with regard to personnel to the board. Although a CSA will look for advisement and guidance from the board attorney, it is important that the trustees are made to understand that there is certain, specific information that cannot be disclosed to them in order to maintain a strict confidence when affording an employee her due process in the event that the board needs to make an unbiased decision or take a formal action regarding her employment and/or tenure in district.

With this, the trustees must be reassured, during multiple times throughout a CSA's tenure in the position, that the CSA is not neglecting to inform them of important issues dealing with faculty or staff and possibly students as they occur. Rather, in protecting the scope of their duty as trustees, it is essential that they be able to make an informed and educated decision, which has not been tainted by outside influences, rumors, and hearsay, on issues that may affect the livelihood of your individual employees and stakeholder groups.

With regard to pending legal matters in district, an update should be given to the trustees on a monthly basis that includes all current legal cases that have not been settled or decided, outstanding arbitrations and disputes with labor units and employees, and updates to district policies in consideration of the changes and additions in the law and state statute. The CSA, alongside the district counsel, must ensure that names are redacted or initials are used to protect the anonymity of all individual employees and minor children involved.

DIFFUSE A BOARD MEETING ISSUE
BEFORE IT IS PUBLIC

It is imperative that the superintendent continuously knows the "pulse" of the district at all times, especially in consideration of district happenings that may have legal ramifications and directly impact students. Depending on the size of the district, it may not always be possible to visit schools on a consistent basis or check in with all administrators on a daily basis. A successful CSA, however, does have her own method of receiving daily updates on major issues and happenings around district.

Especially in the digital era, electronic correspondence and texting provide an immediate vehicle for passing information along from the administrative team to the superintendent at a moment's notice. It is finding this pulse that will allow a good leader to prepare for his board meeting and shield his trustees from any potential embarrassment, so as not to be "caught" with regard to an issue for which everyone was unprepared. There are several key steps to follow when assuring that the board is protected in a legal sense and giving the perception that the CSA is ahead of the matter at hand when a "hot topic" item may present itself in district:

- Ensure that legal counsel is in attendance and is briefed of the situation.
- Review Parliamentary Procedure and Robert's Rules with the presiding officer.
- Have security present, if needed.
- Have the administrative team or cabinet present at the meeting to listen to comments from public or diffuse potential comments from public.
- Have a statement prepared and read prior to the public comment portion of the meeting with the intention of addressing the situation and offering an update for the community or audience. This will afford a superintendent the

opportunity to answer questions before they are asked and help deflect an emotional response from the public. Further, educating the audience as to why something has occurred or a decision has been made can have a calming effect on individuals whose intention was to challenge the superintendent or board in public.

- Change the venue if more seating or more appropriate accommodations are needed.
- If reporters are present and ask for a comment, comment! Granted that from a legal sense, certain issues cannot be discussed, especially on record; however, if there is a programmatic question or a question relative to decisions made in consideration of the health and welfare of students and staff, then a positive statement in support of the decision-making process and reasoning behind such a decision is much better than leaving the interpretation open to all others because "no comment" is given. Comments to reporters should be brief and always support the true mantra of any superintendent's position—"it's all about our students!"
- Make sure that your attorney does most of the talking if questions about the issue arise. A superintendent does not want to say or report anything that could be a legal misrepresentation or violate the rights of others.

During the public participation portion of a board meeting, there is much latitude given to the public when discussing public employees due to the nature of their service. In consideration of libelous and slanderous comments, elected and appointed public officials are held to higher standards, meaning that public scrutiny "comes with the territory." The public has a right to comment on almost any topic and discuss personnel at their own risk of being sued.

The board has a legal obligation not to divulge any personnel information or have further discussion when being addressed by the public. Further, speaking about or discussing a child during a public comment session is obviously not permitted and unacceptable. If a parent wishes to address a concern specific to her son or daughter, it should be done so through the CSA in accordance with board policy and chain of command. Any discussions relative to programs, events, or general questions about the district can be addressed to support the spirit of transparency you continue to strengthen on a daily basis.

SUMMARY AND FUTURE CONSIDERATIONS

There is much to consider when stepping into the office of superintendent of schools. Choosing a team that "fits" the needs of the district should be the first order of business followed by several audits of district systems, which will help assure that an entry plan includes protocols that provide the greatest feedback of where the district is in consideration of programs, budget, and personnel needs. The relationship between the superintendent and the board trustees is an obvious partnership that must be cultivated and strengthened by proving that the superintendent's knowledge of and command in the position will ultimately lead to success for the entire school community.

More important, the communication and partnership that exist between the superintendent and the board and association attorneys will be the determining factor when situations arise and legal counsel is needed for numerous district situations that involve the welfare of students and personnel.

In addition, consider the following as CSA:

• How often should a superintendent formally meet with the board attorney, auditors, and other key service providers?
• When should board trustees be "briefed" on legal concerns and open cases?
• What cabinet positions are most important to a first-year superintendent?

Chapter 2

Education Law and Policy

The best teachers are those who show you where to look but don't tell you what to see.

—Alexandra K. Trenfor

BOARD POLICY

Board policy and regulations contain the procedures that every chief school administrator (CSA) must follow in making decisions in consideration of personnel, students, and district programs. Formulated with respect to laws and state statutes and in conjunction with the culture and needs of the local community, board policy relates the mission of the district and the children served. Hence, each policy should lead to the greatest potential output in consideration of the success of the students and their futures.

This includes academic and social platforms as well as guidelines to follow when directing school personnel in the everyday program of the schools. Board trustees work alongside their superintendent to create appropriate policies to assist the school's chief in administering the schools. In theory, this is the whole scope of their duty as a board trustee—to make policies to assist the administration in operating the schools. However, we know wholeheartedly that this line gets "blurred," at times. Regardless, policies exist to provide a backbone for the decisions and the procedures a superintendent follows in making these decisions.

Specific to students and child law, policies that determine due process rights, student discipline and code of conduct, health considerations and emergencies, and grading system and academic placement are extremely important when supporting the administration and teachers, as well as the mission of the district set forth by the trustees. In developing policies and regulations that affect the district, the superintendent must ensure that he helps steer decisions by keeping the goal of servicing the needs of his students in mind—at all times.

AFFIRMATIVE ACTION

Affirmative action policies and protocols are put in place to protect against the discrimination of historically protected groups and classes of individuals as well as the discriminatory and egregious consequence based on race, nation of origin, sex, or disability. Each district should (or must by statute) approve an administrator who receives training and/or certification as an affirmative action officer (AAO) for the school district who monitors, mediates, and suggests further actions relative to board policy and federal laws.

Most common, besides race and religious claims, are those of sexual harassment, in which individuals are offended by comments or actions in the workplace by other employees. The action doesn't have to be against the complainant herself; rather, any individual present and offended by said allegation may report the occurrence to the AAO for further deliberation. The first consideration of any affirmative action complaint includes a discussion and "apology" by the offender to the offended. In many cases, there is no deliberate attempt to hurt an individual or cause unwarranted stress or anguish due to one's actions, words, gestures, and so forth.

At times, the argument needs to be mediated, and in severe circumstances, the action was so egregious that the investigation warrants further review and additional complaints filed. As CSA, there are three major considerations to follow with regard to affirmative action in your district:

1. Ensure that policies and procedures are updated and include federal or state laws and applicable definitions for all terms.
2. Confirm and document that all faculty and staff have reviewed district policies and receive appropriate training on affirmative action and the complaint process.
3. Ensure that the AAO documents each case and includes any mediation steps agreed to by the parties.

If an affirmative action complaint is alleged on the CSA, it is appropriate to contract with an outside, independent counsel or affirmative action mediator to conduct the investigation, interviews, and so forth. This is important in that there can be no allegation of bias in the investigative process, nor can there be an indication that the chief administrator in some way attempted to circumvent the protocols established by the board of education.

HARASSMENT, INTIMIDATION, AND BULLYING

Some argue that certain forms of bias or malcontent expressed through bullying and harassment mean favoring one group of learners. Rather, calling anyone from those groups, who are being harassed, a "protected class" sounds as if such lists protect some children over others. Of course, this is not the case. Instead, these classes provide a safety net for every student.[1] Harassment, intimidation, and bullying (HIB) is identified when the incident is based on race, national origin, color, sex, age, disability, or religion. When bullying and harassment overlap, schools have an obligation to resolve the issue at hand.[2] Anyone can report (and should report) harassing conduct to the school administration. When a complaint is received, certain steps must be used to investigate and solve for the situation at hand. This occurs by performing the following:

- Immediate and appropriate action should be taken to investigate or otherwise determine what happened.
- Inquiry must be prompt, thorough, and impartial.
- Interview targeted students, offending students, and witnesses, and maintain written documentation of the investigation.

When an investigation reveals that harassment has occurred, school officials must take steps to:

1. end the harassment;
2. remove a hostile environment;
3. prevent the harassment from recurring;
4. prevent retaliation against the targeted student or individual reporting the claim;
5. communicate with targeted students regarding steps taken to end the harassment; and
6. check with targeted students to ensure that the harassment has ceased.[3]

The final step, checking with students to ensure that the issue has been rectified, is a very important step in the process, and one that is most often neglected. A superintendent must ensure that principals, directors, and others involved with antibullying campaigns communicate with student complainants and offenders after the investigation and determinations are complete.

One of the greater issues faced is not if bullying has occurred but what the school's role should be if cyberbullying and other forms of intimidation outside school have taken place (Table 2.1). It is the school administration and antibullying specialist's responsibility to investigate and mediate any possible harassment, intimidation, and suspected bullying that have occurred on school grounds and any HIB activity that has occurred off school grounds if it has carried over and in some way disrupted the educational process.

Table 2.1 States with Bullying Laws and Policies[4]

State	Antibullying Laws and Policies	Cyberbullying	Groups Identified
Alabama	Y	Y	None
Alaska	Y	N	None
Arizona	Y	Y	None
Arkansas	Y	Y	None
California	Y	Y	None
Colorado	Y	N	None
Connecticut	Y	Y	None
Delaware	Y	Y	None
Florida	Y	Y	None
Georgia	Y	Y	None
Hawaii	Y	Y	None
Idaho	Y	Y	None
Illinois	Y	Y	None
Indiana	Y	N	None
Iowa	Y	Y	None
Kansas	Y	Y	None
Kentucky	Y	Y	None
Louisiana	Y	Y	None
Maine	Y	Y	None
Maryland	Y	Y	None
Massachusetts	Y	Y	None
Michigan	Y	Y	None
Minnesota	Y	Y	None
Mississippi	Y	Y	None
Missouri	Y	Y	None
Montana	N	N	None
Nebraska	Y	Y	None
Nevada	Y	Y	None
New Hampshire	Y	Y	Individual student's perceived or actual characteristics, behaviors, or beliefs, as well as harassment that is motivated due to a student's association with another individual and based on that other individual's perceived or actual characteristics or behaviors

(Continued)

State	Antibullying Laws and Policies	Cyberbullying	Groups Identified
New Jersey	Y	Y	
New Mexico	Y	Y	
New York	Y	Y	
North Carolina	Y	Y	
North Dakota	Y	Y	
Ohio	Y	Y	
Oklahoma	Y	Y	
Oregon	Y	Y	
Pennsylvania	Y	Y	
Rhode Island	Y	Y	
South Carolina	Y	Y	
South Dakota	Y	Y	Specifically restricts identifying groups
Tennessee	Y	Y	
Texas	Y	Y	
Utah	Y	Y	
Vermont	Y	Y	
Virginia	Y	Y	
Washington	Y	Y	
West Virginia	Y	Y	
Wisconsin	Y	Y	
Wyoming	Y	Y	

TITLE I

A Title I program is a method of delivering services in eligible schools to assist the schools in addressing the educational needs of students living in a community with an economically disadvantaged student population of 40 percent or greater. Title I services most often provide strategies for improving the entire school environment where every student can attain a high level of academic proficiency in all subject areas.

Schoolwide programs determine how a school can organize Title I programs and allocate the funding sources that are available, including salaries and equipment. Schoolwide Title I programs do not have to identify children as eligible for services and do not have to limit funding strategies to mathematics and English Language Arts (ELA). While schoolwide programs serve all children in the school, targeted assistance Title I programs identify subgroups of learners in specific areas (ELA and mathematics) and advance ancillary programs to help remediate learners.

Staff and resources utilized under Title I are part of the overall purpose to meet and exceed high levels of academic proficiency in core subject areas for all students, especially those most in need in consideration of socioeconomic status. This is achieved by assuring that the parameters of a Title I program include quality instruction, programs based on scientific research, strategies, and methodologies to improve teacher professional development, and a consolidated use of budget funds. Title I teachers utilize data from different assessments and classwork to determine those individual students showing the greatest need for Title I services. Students showing the greatest need who do not have an individualized education program (IEP) receive services first.

SECTION 504[5]

Many parents of children with a physical or mental disability look to a child study team to help their son or daughter receive appropriate accommodations that will be beneficial to his or her success in a school setting. These accommodations are based on goals that are established by the parent and members of the team, and they include anything from a one-to-one aide and additional time on task to test modifications, transportation, and assistive devices (e.g., computer, FM station for hearing impaired, manipulatives). However, in order to receive any accommodations, the child must first meet the definition of having a qualified disability for services pursuant to federal law. By definition, Individuals With Disabilities Education Act (IDEA) lists thirteen specific disability categories in which a child may be approved for services under special education. These categories include:

- autism,
- deafness,
- deaf-blindness,
- hearing impairment,
- intellectual disabilities,
- multiple disabilities,
- orthopedic impairment,
- other health impairment,
- serious emotional disturbance,
- specific learning disability,
- speech or language impairment,
- traumatic brain injury, and
- visual impairment, including blindness.[6]

When students do not qualify for an IEP for special education services due to the definitions prescribed by these categories, they may still qualify for certain accommodations under Section 504 of the Rehabilitation Act of 1973.[7] Qualifying conditions under a 504 plan may include any disability, long-term illness, or disorders that reduce a student's ability to access learning in the educational setting because of a learning, behavior, or health-related condition.[8]

It is important to understand that according to the definition, a physical or mental impairment is not included under Section 504 "unless this impairment creates a substantial limitation to one or more major life activities." The term *major life activities* includes self-care, manual tasks, walking, seeing, speaking, sitting, thinking, learning, breathing, reading, standing, lifting, bending, concentrating, interacting with others, and working.[9]

Thus, as some students have conditions that may be apparent to other students, faculty, and staff, other hidden disabilities may not be as obvious but still limit major life activities and qualify students for accommodations under the law. These conditions include, but are not limited to, diabetes, specific learning disabilities, epilepsy, poor hearing, a chronic illness, heart disease, asthma, and allergies. Regardless of intellect, students with this type of impairment will most likely be unable to fully attain an educational benefit equal to that of a nondisabled student.[10] Conditions relative to environmental, cultural, or economic disadvantage are not part of this definition.

In recent years, accommodations for students with attention-deficit disorder/attention-deficit hyperactivity disorder (ADD/ADHD), dyslexia, cancer, digestive disorders, depression, conduct disorder, HIV, behavior disorders, and temporary disabilities (broken writing arm, etc.) have been made in districts around the country. Students with conditions that are "episodic" or "in remission" are also eligible for accommodations under Section 504 if these conditions create a substantial limitation in one or more major life activity while they are active.[11] Students battling alcohol and/or drug abuse are not eligible under Section 504 for those specific conditions.

In providing accommodations of modifications for students eligible under the tenets of Section 504, teachers and staff must utilize available resources to ensure that these individual students are performing in classes by having equal opportunity as any other student regardless of disability. It is also important to emphasize that faculty and staff members, refusing to make any accommodations for students under this section of the law, may be held personally liable in connection with any lawsuit or relief sought by the parents or individual.

Regardless of a plan under Section 504 or an IEP for classified students, all teachers and staff in primary and supporting roles for said students must acknowledge that they have viewed the plan via their signature on a log to be signed immediately after all parties involved approve the plan.

COMPULSORY ATTENDANCE, TRUANCY, AND HOMESCHOOLING

With the exponential growth of educational access due to specific and certain types of media, the right to education and the ability to transform an educational program to a program that meets the industry standards has become somewhat of a challenge to professionals and parents alike. A specific state's compulsory education laws are meant to deal with those students and families who attenuate a "stock" schedule of minutes and curricular and extracurricular needs so as to neglect certain areas necessary for student success as a twenty-first-century learner.

Truancy and other issues are sometimes related to a student's desire to be homeschooled or seek other alternate methods of education. There continues to be an ongoing battle between the right to education through particular and accredited means and systematic education defined by the traditional sense of the word. No one has braced the fact that education, as challenging as it already is to articulate, becomes nothing less than fractured as we continue to attempt to meet the needs of everyone to ensure that each subgroup of learners is conditioned to succeed.

In fact, compulsory education, homeschooling, and truancy are three important and definitive issues that link together to help establish the basis for public education today, and the responsibility in governing these issues rests in the superintendent's office. Regardless, one may argue that the most important topic, from the standpoint of the success surrounding any student, would be that of the aptitude learned from his program of studies based around a common and succinct core of educational content that includes both informational and societal skills base that can compete with other learners from around the world in a global marketplace.

First enacted in 1853 and 1854 by Massachusetts and New York legislatures, respectively, the compulsory education laws for school attendance came into effect based on the theory that public school systems were the best means and vehicle to improve the literacy rate of the poor while assisting with the assimilation process of an immigrant population that grew at an exponentially high rate between the mid-nineteenth and early twentieth centuries.[12]

Soon after, the remaining states in the union fell "in line" as other causes came to light, including the need to prevent factory owners and industries from exploiting cheap and plentiful child labor. The compulsory education or attendance statutes are enforced by state government and require parents to have their children regularly attend a public or state accredited private or parochial school for a specific duration of time. Each state determines the start and end dates for this period, and most states require a child to begin attending school at an age ranging from five to seven with the ability to stop attending regularly at sixteen or eighteen years of age.

In more modern times, the tenets of the law were used more practically to ensure that students attended school on a regular basis. This ensured that the youth population within the country measured as a whole would keep up with an expanded frontier of advancing fields in technology, also making U.S. students competitive with students from countries around the world who are advancing in the global marketplace. Compulsory attendance laws bind those students who would not attend school otherwise. Since we are discussing minors, many states relate much of the law toward adults or those guardians of the minor children in question.

Failure to comply with the law is a misdemeanor in almost every state where penalties include fines for the first offense ranging from $25 to $100 and increasing thereafter to $1,000 depending upon the jurisdiction. Most states also have the option of sentencing parents for as long as thirty days to jail. Some states provide for alternatives such as community service or counseling.[13] Most state and local judges will refrain from enforcing these laws against parents whose children are physically or mentally disabled, are employed to help benefit the family, or are past the minimum age to "drop out."[14] Judges have also upheld exemptions such as the following:

- A threat to the health, safety, or welfare of a student if the parents can show the threat is imminent.
- The child becomes mentally or physically disabled. However, this ground is now used less frequently because of special services for the disabled mandated by federal law.
- The parents object to classes because the content violates their religious beliefs or practices.
- Either hazardous conditions are present "between the child's home and his designated public school or the distance between the student's home and the school exceeds a distance provided by statute."[15]

TRUANCY

Truancy is the "sister" definition to the compulsory education laws. It is the reasoning behind why these laws are needed in the modern-day educational field. Many parents deal with truancy issues of their children by working with the local school and government officials and incorporate ways in which the adolescent can stay involved in the everyday component of school life. Other parents have given up, considering their children as lost to "the streets" and not affected by what their future will hold.

Absenteeism can lead to low academic achievement, school dropout, student delinquency, and gang-related involvement. School districts that have established "multi-systemic approaches and policies pertaining to student absenteeism" typically experience fewer numbers of dropouts and a greater number of graduates.[16] New Jersey's compulsory education law (N.J.S.A. 18A:38–28 through 31) requires all children between the ages of six to sixteen to attend school, while California requires children between six and eighteen years of age to regularly attend school, with an exception for those seventeen- and eighteen-year-old individual students who have graduated from high school or passed the California High School Proficiency Exam (CHSPE) along with permission from a parent to leave school.

Most state departments of education monitor attendance regulations and require each district board of education to develop, adopt, and implement policies and procedures regarding the attendance of students, including the adoption of a definition of "unexcused absence," and the provision of mandated services for students with between one and nine cumulative unexcused absences and a mandated court referral for truant students, those with ten or more cumulative unexcused absences.[17]

As compulsory education laws require children to attend a public or state accredited private school for a certain period of time, states like New Jersey have, with the implementation of executive county superintendents and the like, strengthened their ability to patrol this situation very carefully. As an example, New Jersey legislature under the compulsory education law (N.J.S.A. 18A:38–25) provides for an adolescent to receive "equivalent instruction elsewhere than at school," including the home. The law goes on, requiring that

> every parent, guardian or other person having custody and control of a child between six and 16 to ensure that such child regularly attends the public schools of the district or a day school in which there is given instruction equivalent to that provided in the public schools for children of similar grades and attainments or to receive equivalent instruction elsewhere than at school.

The provision "to receive equivalent instruction elsewhere than at school" in N.J.S.A. 18A:38–25 permits a parent or guardian to educate the child at home.[18]

Further, parents may opt to pursue Equivalent Education, which may be obtained in a state accredited private school or a parochial school. According to a ruling by the U.S. Supreme Court in *Pierce v. Society of Sisters*, 268 U.S. 510:

> States must recognize these schools as providing an education equivalent to that of the public schools so long as they follow state laws and regulations that bear a reasonable relationship to the interest the state has in educating its citizens and do not burden the religious practices of the parochial schools. These conditions placed upon non-public schools, including home schools, are permitted under the United States Constitution because the public schools must follow these regulations as well.[19]

All nonpublic schools must qualify under the laws of that state as "schools" in order to be considered capable of providing an equivalent education. The states have solidified a "litmus test" that includes the following areas of education that must be present in order to fall under the court's ruling:

- the quality of the teaching;
- the soundness of the curriculum;
- how many hours per day are spent for instruction;
- how many days of the year the school is engaged in teaching; and
- whether the teachers are certified.[20]

Private and parochial schools have to comply with all of these factors of the litmus test.

There are also several common factors that people believe can cause a student not to attend a public institution, including:

- incompetency of teachers;
- a parent's belief that the school is not providing an appropriate education for his child; and
- objections to integration based on religious reasons.

These are topics that are of major concern but not any reason to remove or detain a student from receiving a public education. Any of these would create an immediate need to meet with the public school's administration and even request a formal board of education meeting.

HOMESCHOOLING

Also termed *home education*, *homeschooling* is the education of children inside the home, as opposed to the formal layout of a public or private school in consideration of classrooms, labs, gymnasiums, and other curricular and extracurricular spaces. A parent or, at times a tutor, usually conducts homeschooling.

This does not correlate to what is known as home instruction, which is home education established and scheduled by the school district to take the place of classes due to a medical or disciplinary leave. However, despite its name, only a portion of home education for homeschooling may be delivered in the actual home with physical education, home economics, and other elective courses provided within the local community or alternate sites.[21]

If you think about it, prior to the compulsory education laws circa 1800, all students were homeschooled. The community raised "its" children through the introduction of specific jobs necessary for survival and fruitful living. With modern times came schooling and other initiatives to maintain an adolescent's need for more education and a parent's desire to provide the best opportunities that she could for her children. Usually, the main reasoning behind homeschooling includes parents' disapproval with the local schools or their desire to be more involved with their child's education and development.

Dissatisfaction with schools includes concerns about the school environment, the quality of instruction and personnel who are delivering it, the curriculum, concerns with bullying, and parents' lack of belief that schools are equipped to care for a child with special needs. Parents may choose to homeschool to have a greater influence on what their children are learning; to better prepare their individual aptitude and abilities; to provide for specific religious or moral instruction and beliefs; and to take advantage of one-to-one instruction around a "free" schedule allowing a child to spend more time on childhood activities, socializing with peers, and nonacademic learning.[22]

While the "roots" of education in America are related to home and family initiatives, the homeschooling "movement" arose as a reaction against the public educational system. This is dramatic growth given that the number of students homeschooled in the United States was estimated at only 300,000 in 1990[23] and has grown to nearly 1.6 million school-aged students estimated for the 2017–2018 school year.[24]

The increase reflects a growing dissatisfaction with formal education[25] and a growing public acceptance of homeschooling.[26] Homeschooling can be an option for families living in isolated locations (rural), visiting countries abroad, and for those who must travel on a frequent basis. Many young athletes, actors, and musicians are taught at home so as to better accommodate training and practice schedules, whereas some parents and education experts see homeschooling as a means of mentorship and apprenticeship where a tutor or teacher is with the child for many years and truly knows the child's strengths and weaknesses.

Homeschooling has increased in popularity in the United States where the percentage of children from five to seventeen years of age who are home-schooled increased from 1.7 percent in 1999 to 2.9 percent in 2007.[27] Further, academic statistics when comparing public to homeschooled children point to the single conclusion that homeschooling works. Even the state departments of education, which are generally biased toward the public school system, cannot argue that not only does homeschooling work but it also works without the myriad of state controls, standardized assessments, unfunded mandates, and accreditation standards imposed on the public schools.[28]

However, the downside of allowing the spirit of the compulsory education law to subside includes that of the social aspect of a student attending an institution with his peers. Academics aside, the environment that is education itself consists of an extracurricular component engaged to help adolescents prepare for the nuances of adulthood and relationships. Recently, home-schooling parents have established networks and utilized social media to explicitly work on this area of socialization, almost urging that yes, this is an area lacking in the program.

As a homeschool "curriculum" takes out almost all of the possible distractions, what "real life" job actually does that? This is not to say that homeschooled students are maladjusted; rather, their adjustment period is different from that of their peers creating several other issues that must not go overlooked.

Superintendents should collect "notes" or a promissory explanation from parents who wish to homeschool a child. Further, each board of education should adopt a local policy reflecting a mandated code or the protocols that exist when a child is homeschooled. On the other hand, students who wish to return to school after being homeschooled for several years must be returned to the class and grade that meets their age criteria unless a lack of aptitude and knowledge of basic skills is present. The superintendent can utilize a standardized test equivalency, in-house assessment, or a combination of assessments to measure whether or not this returning student can enter the age-appropriate grade.

Based on all the information obtained, if it is the final decision of the superintendent to place the child in a class below his appropriate age level, the superintendent must make absolutely certain she has given the student enough assessments to make an informed determination. Further, she must feel assured that she has the appropriate documentation, including a strict rationale and evidence supporting her decision. Be reminded that as a caveat to the determination, this decision can always be attenuated and a student promoted should he show signs of major progress during classes.

In all, the effects of the compulsory education laws, homeschooling, and truancy issues intertwine to create an interesting combination that defines a certain access to education and decision-making protocols from the office of the superintendent. As the compulsory laws were created to establish the necessary impetus that education of children was the only way to ensure and secure a successful future, these laws gave "permission" for a free society to choose how a child is educated as long as the choice met specific criteria. In turn, the laws ensured that, on the other end of the spectrum, those individual adolescents who refused to attend school would place their parents at risk of misdemeanor charges with associated fines and penalties.

OPTING OUT OF FEDERAL ASSESSMENTS

There is much opinion about statewide standardized assessments in consideration of monitoring student proficiency levels and engaging in intellectual debates with regard to student advancement and rank comparison among districts within a state and across the nation. Unfortunately, these assessments do not provide an explanation for the plethora of factors that impact a specific district in ranking higher or lower than other districts taking the same assessment. These factors include, but certainly are not limited to, socioeconomic status, special education student rates, per pupil expenditures and below adequacy spending, English Language Learners, and student and teacher migration levels.

Regardless, including both "in-house" testing assessments and standardized assessments provides the CSA and his team with aggregate data necessary to help grow and enhance lessons and differentiate instruction for learners within each individual classroom. The supported data provides the superintendent with a breakdown of proficiencies in consideration of specific subgroups with a concentration on district schools and even individual teachers. As this is an important method for supplying data to instructional staff, the most valid prescription is to do everything possible to ensure that all students take part in the assessments.

It is also important to understand the right of a parent to have his child "opt-out" of taking these assessments. The Every Student Succeeds Act mandates 95 percent test participation, but each individual state has the ability to decide what to do if a school or district does not reach the 95 percent attendance requirement. At this time, no school or district has ever lost federal funding because of opt-outs; however, the federal mandate maintains the requirement that assessments be administered to at least 95 percent of all students. The act allows states to establish their own laws governing "opt-outs" and requires parents to be notified regarding their children's participation rights in assessments (Table 2.2). Consequences for schools that miss this threshold are determined by states and districts.[29]

Table 2.2 States with student "opt-out" for test assessments

State	Opt-Out	Notes
Alabama	N/I^	
Alaska	N/I	
Arizona	No	
Arkansas	No	Unless state board approves request
California	Yes	
Colorado	Y/N*	Start board exempts penalty for under 95%
Connecticut	No	Minor exceptions for health and religious reasons
Delaware	No	Exceptions for extreme medical and mental health conditions
Florida	No	
Georgia	N/I	
Hawaii	No	
Idaho	N/A	District can determine
Illinois	No	
Indiana	Y/N	Not against the law but students need to take assessment to graduate
Iowa	No	
Kansas	Yes	Determined at local level
Kentucky	No	
Louisiana	Yes	
Maine	N/I	
Maryland	No	Lawsuit is pending
Massachusetts	No	
Michigan	Yes	
Minnesota	Y/N	
Mississippi	No	
Missouri	No	
Montana	N/I	
Nebraska	Y/N	
Nevada	Yes	
New Hampshire	No	Exceptions for health conditions
New Jersey	Yes	Not encouraged
New Mexico	No	Exceptions for health conditions
New York	No	
North Carolina	No	

(Continued)

Table 2.2   (Continued)

State	Opt-Out	Notes
North Dakota	N/I	"Opt-out" legislation currently introduced
Ohio	No	
Oklahoma	No	
Oregon	No	Minor exceptions for health and religious reasons
Pennsylvania	No	Minor exceptions for health and religious reasons
Rhode Island	No	Exceptions for health conditions
South Carolina	No	
South Dakota	No	English Language Learners are exempt
Tennessee	N/I	Exceptions for health conditions
Texas	No	
Utah	No	
Vermont	No	Exceptions for health conditions; personal emergencies
Virginia	No	
Washington	Yes	
West Virginia	N/I	
Wisconsin	Yes	(grades 4, 8, and 9–11 only)
Wyoming	No	

Source: Aragon, S., Rowland, J., & Wixom, M. A. (2015, February). Assessment opt-out policies: State responses to parent pushback. Education Commission of the States—ECS Education trends.

^N/I—Information not available
*Y/N—Law is ambiguous (see notes)

In the field of education, there are many links and gaps between the research presented and the practice shown by those individual instructors in the field. There is a strong belief of putting the "theory into practice," where pedagogical considerations can be utilized to strengthen instruction and grow student learning. Specific initiatives, whether state or federally mandated or homegrown, are implemented and adjusted to fulfill some distinct need that has been evidenced by data where a drive to strengthen proficiency is enhanced by indicators put in place to meet educational targets.

These protocols, established to help not only justify the proponents of learning initiated for classroom productivity but also enhance proficiency for students in comparison to an educational mission that transcends throughout a global awareness, are unfortunately driven by an accountability system tasked to ensure teacher productivity is a catalyst for student growth and progress. Thus, in lies the problem. As we assess students on specific core concepts in learning, and therefore assess teachers based on the performance of those students, are we creating a vacuum of autonomy and learning where teachers are "teaching to" high-stakes assessments and not the individual needs of learners?

The educational issue deals with those members of the educational teaching staff in any K–12 district where too many mandates regarding students and education cause teachers to feel that they no longer have autonomy to teach materials and context that they feel are important to their own students. The problem exists because the profession screams of accountability, and with each new administration comes new paradigms. Unfortunately, since there is accountability at all levels and the top-down hierarchical model of most, if not all, education systems continuously changes due to personnel, politics, and pursuits of educational prowess, autonomy may not be realized again for some time.

There is much evidence to support that this problem is a real issue in the field of education. Teacher morale is low, and students are learning only standards relative to testing materials. Ancillary life skills, which should be honed in classrooms, need to be mastered and are lacking due to a diminished autonomy in teacher lesson planning.

Data from national surveys regarding teacher time on task and curricular areas reveal that there is a movement away from teacher creativity and a complacency seen with the utilization of "boiler-plate" segments to ensure compliance. Hence, the nature of knowledge, in which specific bonds between teachers and students help encode different approaches to learning, is seriously affected.[30] As the problem identified directly relates to the lack of teacher autonomy in lesson planning due to assessments or mandates, it is important to evidence that autonomy is a major tenet of the teaching profession.

Teacher preparation programs and licensing guidelines ensure that those individuals, entering the field of education, are duly prepared and well qualified to meet the academic goals set forth by state-specific departments of education and local education agencies. In reviewing those parameters established by licensing bureaus and commissioned by state departments of education, there is an underlying level of professionalism that is further implied for those entering the field (or more of a "calling") of educational instruction. Autonomy is not a right for teachers; rather, it must be earned.[31]

Experience is also a variable that affects how much autonomy teachers have where even highly qualified novice teachers may welcome supervision and administrative support.[32] Novice teachers more clearly identify interpersonal support as influential when compared to the self-efficacy beliefs of "rookie" and veteran teachers.[33] Even though the research demands that programs with fewer experienced teachers will have less autonomy, even veteran educators find themselves "teaching to the test" to ensure student growth rates and proficiency levels meet the expectations of the test-makers and not always the mission and vision set forth by the district.

Court-Related Case Summary:
Harassment, Intimidation, and Bullying

Hector F. v. El Centro Elementary School District, D064035

Hector F., the plaintiff, claims his son was bullied based on physical or educational disabilities citing that he is within a protected class under government and education code. The plaintiff requested that the school district be mandated to comply with the requirements of the discrimination, harassment, and intimidation laws. The initial judgment to dismiss the plaintiff's claims was reversed and remanded where the trial court upheld that the father, as both the guardian and a taxpayer of the district, had standing to seek enforcement of the laws where an identified public and private interest are evidenced, and that the father's argument alleges a breach of mandatory duty for the defendant school district.

Court-Related Case Summary: Compulsory Education

Jonathan L. v. Superior Court of Los Angeles, B192878

Like most states, California compulsory education laws call for a child to be enrolled in and attend a public school full time throughout the day unless the child is enrolled in a private school, is tutored by a person holding a valid state teaching license, or other statutory exemptions in the California Education Code. In a dependency proceeding involving whether parents could legally "homeschool" their children, the motion to homeschool was denied where parents failed to demonstrate that any of the applicable exemptions applied to their children.

SUMMARY AND FUTURE CONSIDERATIONS

Legal and practical issues confronting education in America include the boundaries between public and private education (charter schools, etc.), the constitutional and statutory rights of students and teachers, and the structure of educational governance, including the role of the federal government, local control, and powers of the school board. As the demands of education on global success continue to span the nation, laws and policies spotlighting educational trends and needs of individual learners continue to grow capturing the principles that outline the true definition of education that we all consider the paradigm in education today. Compulsory education needs, individualized programs, and modifications for those individual students who need special care, as well as dealing with bullying and changing cultural trends, are daily considerations for the district superintendent.

In addition, consider the following in education law and policy:

- Which board policies will you review first as a new superintendent in district?
- What programs for students and professional development for teachers are offered in district for HIB?
- Do you have policy for student opt-outs?

Chapter 3

Child Welfare and Policy

Children who have strong, healthy foundations are free to blossom, grow, and soar.

—Randi G. Fine

Federal and state laws are in place to protect children from abuse, neglect, and other forms of maltreatment. Pursuant to these laws, there are mandatory reporting laws and liability issues of which the superintendent must be aware. The superintendent and his staff have a responsibility to report all signs of child neglect or abuse to the division of family services and the local police authorities. This isn't a choice; rather, both agencies must be contacted.

The research of Hubner and Wolfson (1996) found that society needs to make a commitment to better the lives of families, to make somebody else's children all our children.[1] Chief school administrators (CSAs) are aligned with such a field where necessity is only an outlier to measures that must stand firm in order to protect those who need our help the most. Superintendents must utilize district policies, appropriate state statutes, and state and federal laws to make the most informed decision.

The child welfare system includes a group of services designed to promote a safe environment for children, a sense of permanency, and a commitment to strengthen services to families to care for their children. Further, the system successfully provides services through funding of programs and legislative initiatives.

CONFIDENTIALITY AND THE RIGHTS OF THE MINOR

A sitting superintendent of schools should have a sign posted on the wall visible at a moment's notice that reads, "Although I am not responsible, I am

45

to blame." This is especially true in schools regarding the confidentiality of minors and the role of faculty and staff. A successful superintendent must not only ensure that she fully understands the tenets of the laws in this area, but the staff members are also fully trained in the "cans" and "cannots" that hover over this category and the day-to-day operations that impact a district and the office of the superintendent of schools.

The overwhelming importance of maintaining confidentiality within a person–practitioner relationship has been recognized since the fourth century BC and remains one of the fundamental rules of professional ethics and legal issues today.[2] However, in dealing with minors, there is a constant struggle that includes the "fine line" between what makes an individual an "adult" and what is considered the minor age cutoff. As a society, are we to claim that an individual person who turns eighteen years of age is capable of a more appropriate decision-making process than that same individual just forty-eight or seventy-two hours earlier? There isn't some switch that turns "on" at age eighteen, but it is this paradigm that must be used for consistency among different cultures of individuals in a particular society.

When and where do the needs of a minor supersede the rights of the parent? Most youth agencies believe that access to confidential services is necessary since many teens will not seek care if a parent must be told or a health professional requires a parent's consent. English argues that "minors' consent laws are extremely important . . . they encourage young people to seek the health care services they need and enable them to talk candidly with their providers."[3]

Conversely, advocates of parental involvement laws argue that an individual minor's consent reflects "nonchalance" about the actions and the involvement of family while condoning sexual and other types of poor decision-making activities. Even so, those adolescents who seek the benefit of mental health relief and services from a professional, such as school nurses, counselors, and substance abuse coordinators, are looking for an advocate by reaching out since there are teens whose parents are not their best advocates.[4]

Laws and policies are put forth to protect the privacy rights of all members of society from the unwilling release of confidential materials and should only be divulged to particular individuals by the individual. This particularly becomes a more interesting topic when we discuss the mental and physical state of those individuals who fall under the category of "minor" children. In deciding on a policy regarding confidentiality, healthcare professionals must prioritize the patient's autonomy and level of maturity, the trust in the provider-patient relationship, the family dynamics as they exist, respect for the parent, and potential short- and long-term consequences of upholding or breaching confidentiality.

Regardless, as in any situation there may be circumstances in which deviation from the policy is essential. The professional must remember that her obligation is to the individual and that as a fiduciary of the individual, she must seek to protect and promote that individual's privacy and health-related interests.[5]

In school systems, students who are less than eighteen years of age, unless officially emancipated, fall under the supervision of a parent or guardian. Hence, parents have the right to all information regarding school district policies and regulations (e.g., grades, attendance, discipline record, transcript), but specific laws still govern the confidentiality standards as established for protected health- and counselor-related interactions.

Take for example the case of a student, eighteen years of age, who is caught with a large amount of marijuana in the school restroom. As policy may dictate, the principal or superintendent files a police complaint and presses charges on the student. Though he is eighteen years old, the police arrests and processes him without his parent's knowledge, since he is considered an adult. Regardless, the discipline policy directs the administration to contact the parent or guardian and levy a suspension based on a serious infraction of the district disciplinary code. Here, we see how the school protocols usurp the methods of legal procedure, in that, parents are still responsible for the actions of their children while not emancipated in a school setting. However, be aware that no matter what is established in the law, the superintendent in his office must always err on the side of caution and for the safety of the student, students, and/or staff for which he is responsible. This is an extremely vast responsibility.

Although it is an unwritten rule, every state has a different definition on the rights of minors to withhold information from parents or guardians or give consent without the knowledge of a parent or guardian. This specifically holds true for permitting minors to consent to general medical treatment where less than one-fifth of U.S. jurisdictions have a broad, mature, minor exception to the standard requirement of parental consent. The remainder either have no exception at all to the rule (34[6]), significantly narrower versions of the law, or specifically permit minors of any age to consent to treatment in all or specific circumstances.[7]

Many states do permit minors to consent for outpatient mental health services. The statutes in these states contain limitations with respect to the age of minors who may consent, the type of care that may be provided, the healthcare professionals who are covered, and the number of visits for which a minor may be seen without the involvement of a parent. For instance, in New Jersey, there are no specific laws addressing whether or not a minor can seek mental health services without the consent of a parent or guardian.[8] The areas that are somewhat defined are still very gray. However, the state legislature is actively pressing that considerations for minors receiving treatment without parental consent be given with regard to mental health issues along with other specific health-related issues already garnered by state law.

This is an extremely important consideration since it is said that a fear of disclosing all information because of parental involvement may prevent some minors from seeking healthcare services, but when young people are assured that their healthcare providers and school nurses will respect their privacy and keep their medical and mental health records confidential, they are comfortable receiving healthcare services. Further, many laws do not require a provider to disclose medical records relating to reproductive health care to parents without the patient's (student's) consent.[9] For example in New Jersy, such disclosure should only be made when consistent with the confidentiality policies of the practice setting, with professional ethical guidelines, and when it is in the minor's best interest.[10]

The same will soon apply to mental health situations since the idea of "open" communication may not always be possible for all young people in all households. Some teens come from homes in which emotional abuse, sexual abuse, or physical violence is the unfortunate normalcy. Other adolescents may have parents who do not support them in seeking different types of health care due to personal, societal, and even religious reasons.

Health Insurance Portability and Accountability Act

The Health Insurance Portability and Accountability Act (HIPAA)[11] of 1996 Privacy Rule creates the skeletal framework for informed consent and confidentiality rights with regard to minors. When state law permits the minor to consent to a treatment, the minor controls his personal medical information under HIPAA. There are, however, situations where minors are given sole authority to consent to medical treatment, including consent to treatment by virtue of their status (the minor is deemed emancipated or considered an adult for the purpose of medical decision making) and unemancipated minors who may have a decision-making authority in certain contexts, due to their cognitive maturity (the "mature minor" doctrine) or because the minor seeks treatment for certain medical conditions.[12]

Family Educational Rights and Privacy Act

Family Educational Rights and Privacy Act (FERPA)[13] gives parents certain rights with respect to their children's records, unless a school is provided with evidence that there is a court order or state law that specifically prevents it. Otherwise, parents have the right to access their children's education records, have the records amended, the right to consent to disclosure of personally identifiable information from the records, and the right to file a complaint with the Department of Education.

When a student reaches eighteen years of age or attends a postsecondary institution, all rights under FERPA transfer from the parent to the student; however, if the student (after turning eighteen) is still enrolled in secondary school and is considered a dependent child of the parent (based on Section 152 of the Internal Revenue Code), the parent is entitled to educational information, including, but not limited to, grades and disciplinary and other education records.

The term *education records* is defined as those records that contain information directly "related to a student and which are maintained by an educational agency or institution or by a party acting for the agency or institution." This includes health records, counseling records, and other information kept on file.[14]

Supreme Court–Related Case Summary: FERPA

Owasso Independent School District No. I-011, aka *Owasso Public Schools et al. v. Falvo, Parent and Next Friend of Her Minor Children,* Pletan et al. (2002)

In consideration of peer editing as an educational practice, teachers sometimes ask students to score each other's assessments and assignments while the teacher is busy helping other students. Claiming that "peer grading" violates the FERPA of 1974, the plaintiff filed a 42 U.S.C. §1983 action against the school district and school officials. Recall that education records are defined as "records, files, documents, and other materials" containing information directly related to a student, which "is maintained by an educational agency or institution or by a person acting for such agency or institution." The district court held that grades inputted by another student are not considered education records. The circuit court reversed the original decision upon appeal finding under FERPA that grades marked by students on each other's work are "education records." Therefore, peer grading does violate the federal FERPA laws.

True or False? How Knowledgeable Are You With FERPA?[15]

1. Teachers are permitted to post grades with names outside of their classroom door.
2. School nurse records are not subject to FERPA.
3. When a student turns eighteen, parents do not have any rights to obtain education records for their son or daughter.
4. When a student transfers from one school to the next, the sending district must send all education records to the new school under FERPA.

5. FERPA requires education records be maintained for seven years.
6. Records created and maintained by a school resource officer are subject to FERPA.
7. Schools must permit parents to review records within a reasonable time period.
8. Divorced parents both have the right to review education records under FERPA.
9. An "education record" is a record that is directly related to a student and maintained by an educational institution or its designee.
10. Only school officials with an educational purpose are permitted to access education records of students under FERPA.

SUMMARY AND FUTURE CONSIDERATIONS

The welfare and safety of a child is the number one priority for every superintendent of schools. This includes not only physical means but also protections from social and educational wrongdoings. Confidentiality with regard to counseling efforts, information that falls under HIPAA, and educational records protected under FERPA guidelines must be a protected practice within any administration. A superintendent can only rest assured when administrators and personnel are keeping appropriate records confidential.

In addition, consider the following in child welfare and policy:

• What is a records retention schedule, and how long do I have to keep certain records?
• Would your teachers pass the FERPA quiz as well?
• Where are medical records stored in each of your schools?

Chapter 4

Juvenile Justice Law and Policy

> Rehabilitation happens when teenagers are forced to connect to their communities and confront their mistakes.
>
> —Joaquin E. Diaz DeLeon

Law, policies, and practices of the American juvenile justice system are important when strengthening the relationship between local law enforcement and the school superintendent. Juvenile justice law and policy has been shaped by research on adolescent development, including brain research and the ability of adolescents to make mature and informed decisions.

On any given school day, the entire adolescent population of a community may be confined inside a local district's school buildings. Parents charge school officials, teachers, and staff with ensuring that their children are safe and out of harm's way when their children arrive at school each morning. In light of this, education officials must be cautious when making decisions regarding student infractions of the discipline policy versus legal issues involving these actions.

A key strength of a school administrator is knowing the difference between infractions that are the result of poor, adolescent student behavior and actions that should be considered violations of the law. Board policy most likely will dictate when an administrator must involve local law enforcement agencies; however, there are certain acts and infractions of the disciplinary code that may also lead to student involvement with the police and the courts. Arrests made for minor misconduct in schools by students cause the improper involvement of the justice system in school discipline matters.[1]

Since school systems are more familiar with students than the court system, schools are better able to respond to student misbehavior in an individual manner.[2] It is important for the superintendent to know the school climate of

51

each of his buildings and overall district, in consideration of not only the academic program of the schools but also student discipline and school safety. The utilization of climate surveys, stakeholder teams, the school resource officer program, and other student programs that address gang awareness, drinking and driving, drugs, domestic violence, and other adolescent issues creates a proactive campaign to help prevent legal issues for students.

A memorandum of understanding[3] (MOU) with a district's local police department or sheriff and prosecutor's office is essential in providing the working agreement between all parties involved in helping to ensure the safety and success of your district and the overall community. There are some districts where staff, parents, and students find a police presence to be threatening. Officers in local schools are sometimes perceived as undertrained, unfamiliar with adolescent behavior and the effects of peer pressure, and unaccountable.

Further, their presence in the schools and the ability for them to humiliate students by entering classrooms to make arrests can create a sense that these officers are "out of place" when stationed in the halls of learning.[4] The role of the police in any school system must, at all times possible, be limited to helping to foster a school climate that remains positive by respecting students' rights and protecting the school environment.

CRIMINALIZING SCHOOL BEHAVIOR: SCHOOL-TO-PRISON PIPELINE

Over the past twenty years, staff and students in school districts across the nation have experienced a tremendous increase in the number of disciplinary and security measures in their schools,[5] including the adoption of zero tolerance policies for guns and other punitive measures for codes of conduct infractions and the installation of security measures such as metal detectors, surveillance cameras,[6] and school resource officers (SROs).[7] Administrators and teachers alike attempt to utilize school district policies and regulations to administer school discipline and support growth while enhancing academic and social opportunities for all students.

Most district discipline policies today follow a "progressive discipline" initiative that greatly mirrors that of our legal system where penalties for infractions intensify with each subsequent infraction. Policies in recent years seem to have removed the "gray" areas that once helped define the ability to work with students to mediate and solve issues with their peers. Recent mainstream terroristic events, threats in schools, and a heightened urgency for society to conquer criminal behaviors at a young age have caused discipline initiatives that work to stifle behavioral modification by substituting adolescent angst for criminal misconduct. Rather, effective school discipline must be adminis-tered so as to keep students within the school setting at all times throughout the school day.

Whenever possible, infractions of the school discipline policy must be addressed by using "nonpunitive interventions" to help improve school safety and academic performance (e.g., restorative justice, peer mediation, counsel-ing services) and not exclusionary measures or criminal justice interventions.[8] There is a link between school disciplinary practices, school failure, and future criminal involvement, providing clear evidence of the phenomenon known as the "school-to-prison pipeline."[9]

While American schools continue to adopt strict discipline policies and stringent security measures as an effort toward achieving safer schools, these initiatives threaten the nurturing "ideal" perceived by school systems. The adoption of stringent disciplinary and security policies leads to harsher punishments for misbehavior where once discipline handled by teachers now equates to suspensions, expulsions, and arrests.[10] Arresting minor students to control misbehavior damages the school administration's ability to address behavioral issues in a productive way.

Removing a student from school is removing him from the exact environ-ment that can provide him with the assistance needed to correct the apparent misbehavior. Police involvement and subsequent school arrests provide a "direct conduit" for students to the school-to-prison pipeline by making it more likely that even minor acts of misbehavior in school will lead to contact with the justice system.[11] Students who are incarcerated for crimes tend to test two or more years behind their peers in basic skills; have higher rates of grade retention, suspension, absenteeism, and expulsion; and are likely to return from prison or a detention program unskilled and uneducated.

Most incarcerated youth "drop out" of school by age sixteen, and they are 3.5 times more likely to be arrested than their peers who graduate high school.[12] Chief school administrators (CSAs) and members of the admin-istrative team must refrain from "criminalizing" students for inappropriate behaviors that can be handled by mediation techniques, positive behavioral interventions and supports (PBIS),[13] and school disciplinary measures. Administrators, faculties, and staff members need professional development to educate and manage the behavior of students with disciplinary issues. Additionally, school districts must adopt policies requiring that a parent or guardian be present for any questioning of a child whenever possible that criminal charges may be filed.[14]

As of 2010, every public school in America has implemented school secu-rity measures, in one form or another.[15] While schools serving urban, poor, and minority students have often adopted the most punitive policies,[16] this is clearly not only an urban problem. While many of the intensified security and disciplinary measures did first appear in urban school settings,[17] these measures spread to the suburbs after Columbine[18] and an increased drug use by students in schools around the country.[19]

An increased public fear of adolescents has also defined the relationships between schools and their students. Schools have become more "prison-like," resembling fortresses and secured by cameras, metal detectors, and armed and unarmed police officers. School officials claim that this ensures safety, but some parents and child advocates see this type of intervention as a means by which schools may dispose of unwanted children.[20]

Misdemeanors comprise of more than 90 percent of charges against arrested students.[21] Criminalizing school-type offenses keeps children out of the school system and thrusts them into the juvenile justice system. Data suggests that making schools "secure environments" lowers morale and makes learning more difficult.[22]

It is important to involve stakeholder groups when structuring a discipline code for your district. Although policies must contain consequences involving local law enforcement agencies for those infractions that are egregious, against the law, and may endanger lives, day-to-day student conflicts and minor infractions aligned with common adolescent behaviors can undoubtedly be handled with less punitive measures, including counseling, support groups, mediation, and advocacy programs. In turn, this type of behavioral modification system will enhance the educational mission of the school district and greatly minimize the perception of a criminal atmosphere around the schools.

STUDENT THREATS AND PREVENTATIVE DISCIPLINE

Student threats to the safety of oneself or others must be taken very seriously in the school setting. Many districts around the country have adopted zero tolerance policies to ensure that students, faculty, and staff are protected from individuals with weapons or who choose to cause harm to others and disrupt the educational atmosphere of the institution. A superintendent must create and implement a proactive approach for the identification, response, and elimination of any and every threat that is alleged in her district.

In a threat assessment situation, certain protocols must be followed in order to ensure that a consistent paradigm is established and followed among all district employees. A successful model reinforces to all stakeholders:

- that threats made by students must be identified quickly;
- the seriousness of the threat itself and consequent danger the threat poses to others;

- important and useful intervention strategies to reduce the risk of violence; and
- a follow-up method to assess intervention results, receive feedback, and make adjustments to enhance the assessment process.[23]

A threat is a type of expression where there is an intent to do harm or act out violently against a person or thing. A perceived threat can be spoken, written, or symbolic (e.g., making a shooting gun motion with hand or fingers). There are several types of threats that an administrator must be able to define at any given moment:

- A *direct* threat is a specific act against a defined target and is delivered in a straightforward, clear, and explicit manner ("I am going to shoot Mary tomorrow in the gym.").
- A threat that is *indirect* is vague, unclear, and ambiguous. The actual plan, victim, motivating factors, and other aspects of the threat are hidden or unapparent ("I'm so mad, I can shoot up the school!").
- A *veiled* threat implies violence but does not threaten violence ("We would be better off without you around anymore.").
- A *conditional* threat warns that something violent will happen unless demands or certain "terms" are met ("If I don't get an 'A' on my paper, I am going to punch you.").[24]

Threats are usually transient (rhetorical; not genuine expressions of intent to harm) or substantive (express intent to physically injure someone in an immediate measure).[25] It is important for a superintendent to ensure that his administrative team continuously develops professionally with respect to identifying and reacting appropriately to threats from students. Although your building principal and her assistants are on the "front line," the liability for dissolving threats ultimately ends as your responsibility. The flowchart[26] in figure 4.1 outlines the appropriate steps to follow in determining whether a proposed threat is transient or substantive.

A CSA must always consider student and school personnel safety as a top priority. Communication with parents and the public with regard to safety measures, precautions, and procedures creates a positive perception of the district and a healthy assurance to parents who invest the most in your district.

Direct and indirect threats should be accompanied with information sent to parents and the community that explains the threat or issue in general terms; assures student safety; outlines the administrative and local law enforcement response to the threat itself, providing evidence of collaboration and cooperating efforts; and prescribes a caveat proclaiming that actions of this type will not be tolerated by the district administration and local authorities. Without a safe environment, academic success cannot be achieved, and

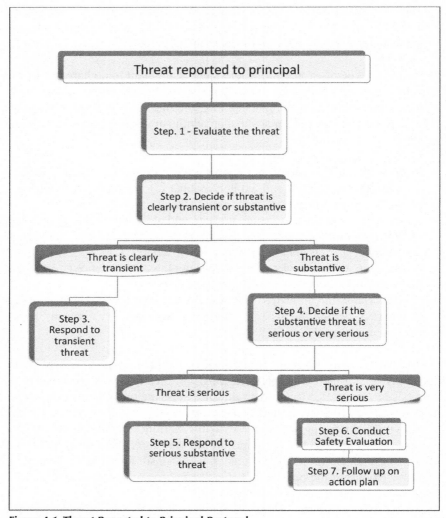

Figure 4.1 Threat Reported to Principal Protocol

quality teacher retention will be nearly impossible to accomplish. In order to meet the needs of a district in consideration of school and student safety against threats, preventative discipline within proactive policies must supplement the superintendent as he:

- creates and "trains" a planning team to research and develop an effective threat assessment program;
- identifies safety roles for school personnel (faculty and staff);

- clarifies the active role of law enforcement in consideration of all threats and the protocols and procedures that will occur with each individual threat (prior to, during, and after the threat has concluded); and
- conducts assessments for those students or individuals who make threats of violence.[27]

THREATS TO TEACHERS

It seems like a simple solution, but dealing with a student who threatens a teacher can be more complicated than expected. Although information and evidence may be gathered with regard to the infraction, each student is afforded his due process in consideration of any and all matters disciplinary in nature. Board policy must be established to support disciplinary protocols, including student expulsion, with regard to threats to school personnel.

Regardless of the due process that is afforded to the individual student and the reports and evidence obtained through administrative and stakeholder witnesses, actions in support (or in rejection) of how district school building leadership team handles the situation will be scrutinized almost immediately and by more than just immediate staff members. Threats to personnel, and specifically teachers, are unacceptable! The ability to manage a classroom safely and efficiently wholly depends on the manner in which that individual manager (teacher in this example) is safe herself. Once that barrier is crossed and a threat fades the line between child and adult, everything in the surrounding environment is affected. This includes not only the safety of the students and individuals directly involved but the educational atmosphere as well.

Moreover, it is clearly understood by other students and individuals in the school or district that if a threat can be made to a teacher and there is no stern discipline present, more threats can be made with no repercussions. Further, a student who receives no consequence for making a threat may likely feel that he can get away with more dangerous infractions in consideration of the code. It is imperative that the CSA shows support for faculty and staff with regard to threats of violence and workplace safety. It is even more important for the CSA to ensure that her leadership team also deals with every issue with this mantra in mind.

Understand that legal statutes and policy will guide you directly in handling this situation. Granted, students deserve and will receive their due process rights in consideration of a thorough investigation into the matters at hand; however, a strong evidentiary presence as to any threat against an employee must be handled in a stern disciplinary manner. It is important to remember how the superintendent and her team respond to the threat, the transparent process throughout the act, and what occurs after it has been established that a threat was made will be scrutinized by all and may affect the course of how future incidents are portrayed and decisions are made. It will also adjust the climate of the faculty and staff for the better or worse.

WEAPONS IN SCHOOL: ZERO TOLERANCE

Weapons have absolutely no place in a school yard or classroom. Although any object that is used to inflict pain or physical harm can be considered a "weapon," for the purpose of this section, a weapon is a knife, gun, or other incendiary object that may be used to threaten or cause bodily damage. There must be zero tolerance for students who bring weapons to school with the intent to endanger another individual student or school personnel.

In establishing policies and procedures to act against individual students who choose to go against a weapons policy, CSAs must follow state and federal statutes as well as other important protocols when advising the board on student disciplinary issues involving weapons:

1. All student matters with weapons must be reported to the police and other executive officers (e.g., county/state superintendents, state monitor).
2. A record and report must be placed on file from the building leadership team (principal) to the CSA. Ensure that this record includes written statements from staff and students who may have witnessed the event and any videos as well.
3. More than likely, a student with an infraction of this magnitude will be placed on long-term suspension while an investigation takes place. This includes a letter to the parents and home instruction or tutoring for students who are out of school for a certain length of time (usually more than three days).
4. Depending on the nature of the incident, parents or community may be notified. Take caution and consult your board attorney in this matter due to the fact that you do not want to release any information or findings pertinent to any case that may need to come before a judge or that you do not offer any information that may harm the offender or negate the offender's due process rights.
5. Ensure that follow-up psychological assessment and counseling sessions are established for these individual students and others affected by the action.

STUDENTS AND DRUGS

The "Say No to Drugs" campaign of the 1980s led to the creation of a national movement of prevention in consideration of school-aged children and the drug epidemic that we continue to face in the United States. From Red Ribbon Week and DARE officers to community and government groups, the movement targeted primary and secondary school students to thwart consumption of illegal substances. Decades later, the nation now faces another battle in the schools with the increase in the use of opioids and performance enhancing drugs in both urban and suburban school settings.

Of the 20.5 million Americans twelve years of age or older who had reported a substance abuse disorder in 2015, nearly 10 percent (2 million) used prescription pain relievers and approximately 3 percent (591,000) involved heroin.[28] The current state of the opioid crisis is exponentially growing to epidemic proportions in certain areas of the country. School district policies and procedures must be in place and in line with local state laws in order to provide prevention, rehabilitation, and discipline for those individual students who use drugs/narcotics and even as important for those innocent students not taking part in the epidemic.

In consideration of this, each infraction must be categorized in separate form with three specific classifications identified as:

* Under the Influence (personnel believes the student is under the influence of drugs or alcohol);
* Possession of a Controlled Substance on School Premises; and
* Possession of a Controlled Substance with an Intent to Distribute.

It is important to understand that with each infraction, effective counseling must be provided and mandated in order to assist in the development of the student and his rehabilitation. Each policy must include a specific outline and protocol in consideration of exact steps to follow and measures to take with regard to the health or safety of the student (school nurse to observe and take vital statistics, etc.), drug testing of the student, disciplinary actions taken, involvement of parents or law enforcement agencies, and reporting considerations to the board and executive offices.

Policy must also dictate what occurs when a student or parent refuses to concede to a drug screen or enter counseling. Most often, this translates into a "guilty" disposition, and the student is subjected to discipline as if being found under the influence. If students are caught with controlled substances on their person in school or at school district–sponsored events/activities, a consideration of expulsion should be given to the individual student, being consistent with past practice, in order to establish a zero tolerance for controlled substances on campus and a strict edict that the safety of innocent students is the number one priority for the CSA.

This especially holds true for those individuals who have been caught with a large quantity of "product" that constitutes an intent to distribute. A strict and stern policy protects those students and staff from the harm that distribution can bring not only from the individual but also from outside sources looking to create a violent atmosphere around the school due to perceived, drug-related interests.

SCHOOL SAFETY TEAMS

As discussed in chapter 2, the superintendent is charged with the final determination and assessment of remediation and disciplinary actions with regard to cases of harassment, intimidation, and bullying (HIB). Further, in creating a strong awareness for the importance of school safety and a positive educational environment, the district leader must look to a stakeholder group to provide oversight of the established policies, practices, and procedures in conjunction with monitoring issues affecting the school climate overall.

In order to take a proactive stance in combating issues surrounding negative influences and HIB, a superintendent establishes protocols and policies to outline the creation of School Safety Teams in every school in the district. School Safety Teams are formed to help foster, develop, and maintain a positive school climate by focusing on the systemic processes in a school while examining school climate issues, including HIB.[29] A School Safety Team meets throughout the school year (usually once per semester), and it includes in its membership the principal or his designee; a teacher; the school antibullying specialist (ABS; usually the "chair" of the committee); a parent who has a child or student in the building; and other members to be determined by the principal.[30]

It is the responsibility of this team to act as a liaison between students and personnel and address matters that can contribute to a hostile work environment. The team further resembles a system of "checks and balances," ensuring that all complaints are reported and recommended and prescribed actions occur in a timely fashion. The team:

- receives all complaints of HIB of pupils that have been reported to the principal;
- reviews reports prepared after an investigation of an incident of HIB;
- identifies patterns of HIB of pupils in the school and makes recommendations to the principal;

- assists in strengthening the climate and policies of the school in order to prevent and address HIB of pupils;
- creates awareness for the entire school community about prevention of HIB of pupils;
- participates in professional trainings to carry out all team requirements pursuant to district policies and state and federal guidelines; and
- works closely with the district antibullying coordinator in collecting district-wide data and adjusting district policies to prevent and address alleged acts of HIB.[31]

A parent member of the school safety team cannot participate in any meeting or decision where the dialogue may compromise the confidentiality of any student.[32]

STUDENT WALKOUTS

There are many national, state, and local issues that may have a direct or indirect effect on the students, faculty, and other stakeholders in your district. These issues can be related to events that have occurred in other states, political decisions and laws under scrutiny by legislators, and nonrenewal of "popular" teachers by the superintendent and board of education. Students may become motivated to take action as a stand for or against some of these situations, and a group of bright and well-organized student activists can make a superintendent and his administration react to anything from a simple demonstration to a student walkout.

The law is clear that students do not have a First Amendment right to unilaterally disrupt the school day by walking out of the building as an act of political protest. Even though district leadership must avoid conduct that could be viewed as a violation of a student's constitutional rights, the superintendent and trustees must act in an appropriate manner to preserve the safety of students, faculty, and staff by providing disciplinary consequences to students who violate the student code of conduct. Hence, if an unauthorized walkout occurs that disrupts the operation of the educational process of the school, then the participating students are not engaged in a constitutionally protected activity, and the administration may use measures to prevent the action or impose discipline for those who engage in it.

As state statutes and the compulsory education laws dictate that school attendance is mandatory where students must be present in school, the district is authorized to discipline students, consistent with its code of student conduct, for violating its policies on attendance, class cutting, and excused and unexcused absences regardless if the violation occurs during some type of political protest like a walkout. The American Civil Liberties Union contends that districts should support students who engage in political activism and not discipline students for political protest. In deciding First Amendment cases, the courts have ruled that suppressing the speech of students is not favored; however, districts are given some latitude in consideration of regulating speech by restricting the time, manner, and place for the exercise of First Amendment rights by students.

A superintendent can work with his administrators to be proactive and dictate that a scheduled act of protest be used as a lesson in civic engagement, as opposed to sanctioning an expected walkout, and at the same time protect his students' rights to free speech by assisting student activists with scheduling safe, alternative activities. This can include assemblies, open forums, town hall–style engagements, and spokespersons. It is critical for any superintendent to understand that arranging something of this nature for one politically charged group of students, the district must be prepared to permit activities spotlighting the counter viewpoint on the same issue or any speech relating to another political issue entirely in the near or distant future. In other words, a superintendent or board cannot decide which group or viewpoint can protest and which others cannot. A prime example includes student protests on gun control in the aftermath of school shootings that occur across the country. If students are permitted to engage in a political action to oppose gun laws, other students must be permitted to argue in favor of gun laws as well.

Should discipline be levied to students, it would violate a student's constitutional rights to impose harsher discipline for a politically motivated code of conduct violation than the discipline that would be imposed for the same conduct that is not politically motivated. So, if the code of conduct calls for a detention for students who walk out of the building unauthorized, only a detention can be given for a student who walks out in protest. The same holds true where a student wearing a T-shirt or article of clothing that expresses a political viewpoint should not be considered disruptive or subject to discipline simply because someone may disagree with the viewpoint. If the clothing constitutes a dress code violation, it should not be treated differently than any other dress code violation.

A superintendent should do everything possible to anticipate political actions taken by students, protests, and walkouts prior to them occurring. It is always best to discuss the possibility of these actions in order to ensure student safety and a positive reaction from the school and community. On one hand, a superintendent can be proud that students are engaging in a civic duty to speak out for their beliefs, a mission of the district in that students are being prepared to take an educated stand for their beliefs and future. On the other hand, a superintendent unprepared for such actions may react in such a way that may be perceived as his attempt to stifle the voices of his students. Obviously, that is not a desired perception for the leader of an educational system.

Court-Related Case Summary: First Amendment

Cuff v. Valley Central School District, 10–22–82

In 1983, elementary school parents claimed that their child's First Amendment rights under the U.S. Constitution were violated by the district when the child was suspended from school after "wishing" for violence to the school itself and teachers. This was communicated in a "drawing exercise." The school's discipline was upheld by the court citing that it could easily have been concluded that the drawing would disrupt the educational process.

SUMMARY AND FUTURE CONSIDERATIONS

School leaders, and specifically the district CSA, have the responsibility and an obligation to enforce the school code of conduct in order to maintain a positive and safe school environment and not disrupt the educational pipeline. There must be zero tolerance for violence, weapons, drugs, and the like in consideration of protecting innocent student victims from those students looking to harm themselves and others.

On the other hand, district officials must also be careful and not be so quick to criminalize all student behaviors that fall under the student code of conduct. Doing so lessens the effective discipline waged on more serious offenses and involves police and local authorities in issues that could be handled "in house." Superintendents and CSAs ensure that school building leaders recognize that students are adolescents and make mistakes every day. Only repeat offenders and those with a premeditated pulse to cause some type of damage to the school facilities, culture, and individuals should seek counseling and penalties from higher authorities.

However, a superintendent must not be too quick to judge everything as some type of quick referral to the local juvenile detectives and courts. Granted, some situations must be reported, but the majority should be handled through remedial measures, interactions, and behavioral modifications to assist the student with the life skills necessary to move on from his mistakes and not make the same bad decisions again.

In addition, consider the following in juvenile justice law and policy:

• What is the role of an SRO? What are the parameters of his engagement with students and his assisting with student discipline issues?
• How often would you expect a principal to press charges on students for incidents that occur during a school day? What types of incidents would cause these charges to be filed?

Chapter 5

Family Law and Policy

Family is the most important thing in the world.

—Princess Diana

The legal and social landscape of family law has become an increasingly more important subject in schools and greatly relates to the role of the superintendent. Specific procedures and protocols need to be in place and followed in consideration of custody, visitation of parents, and other issues surrounding immediate and extended family members. Court orders and other considerations put the superintendent and building administrators "in the middle" of family issues and legal considerations. It is imperative that proper documentation is obtained, recorded, and disseminated to personnel directly involved in student issues so that everyone involved is well informed and understands the legal accommodations to be followed with regard to the student.

IN *LOCO PARENTIS V. PARENS PATRIAE*

Both the doctrines of in loco parentis and *parens patriae* are relevant to the school setting. In loco parentis is defined as care that is "temporary in character and not to be likened to [the permanent situation of] adoption."[1] The in loco parentis doctrine can be applied to both schools and nongovernmental entities and is in force when a person or a legal entity undertakes the care and control of another person of legal incapacity in the absence of such supervision by that individual's natural parents and in the absence of any court document or other formal legal approval. Thus, certified administrators and classroom teachers fall under the umbrella of in loco parentis when children are placed in their authority for the length of a school day or duration of a school activity.

Parens patriae is the common law doctrine that regulates custodial authority of adults in the best interest of children. This is public educational authority at its most concise sense. Compulsory schooling laws require all persons having care and control of a child to "share" custody with teachers for limited periods of time knowing that the welfare and developmental interests of every child include access to public knowledge and diverse formative influences. Nowhere is this view more apparent than in legal opinions featuring the terms *parens patriae* and *education* since these are the types of disputes in which the educational interests of children are necessarily implicated.[2]

DIVISION OF YOUTH AND FAMILY SERVICES (CHILDREN AND PROTECTIVE SERVICES)

Protocols must be approved and utilized that provide enough support and documentation for teachers to involve state and local divisions of youth and family services departments in the event that students exhibit or discuss distress in consideration of their "home" and those individuals charged with providing care for them before and after school hours. Commonly known as Division of Youth and Family Services (DYFS) or DCPP, it is imperative that a superintendent and her administrative team ensure that all employees know that it is their right and obligation to report all matters of child abuse or neglect to the appropriate authorities, an administrator, or the chief school administrator (CSA) should they feel any neglect exists.

As a memorandum of understanding is developed with a local police department or law enforcement agency, it may be also decided that the police are informed every time that a student situation is referred to DYFS. This doesn't insist that the police need to respond to the school building; rather, it is a means by which your faculty and staff affirm that there is documented proof that school personnel have some concern about the welfare of a pupil. All school administrators must log each announced DYFS "call" and submit it to the board office (superintendent's office or designated official) for approval and record-keeping purposes. Redaction or initials can be used to protect the names of individual students and teachers; however, it is important to recognize that should a case become active and reach the courts, nothing remains confidential. It is always better to err on the side of caution if one is unsure as to whether or not to inform DYFS. Let the caseworker make the decision for you after you refer the issue to your local division office.

INSTITUTIONAL DYFS

At times, you may receive a report from a building administrator outlining a concern with regard to alleged neglect or abuse against a student by a teacher or professional staff member. Besides your normal investigative routine, most states have an institutional DYFS that handles situations of this nature. The caseworker will advise you of her findings and any additional procedures you must follow based on state and federal guidelines.

The outcome of the findings may result in further investigation and disciplinary action for faculty and staff. An action plan may need to be put in place in order to ensure that an incident of this nature will not be a recurring matter in the district, and all outliers have been mediated.

DIVORCE AND CUSTODY

Divorce and concerns over custody always include fragile conversations with parents and family members. District registrars, compliance officers, and building administrators are empowered as a designee of the CSA to ensure that the district is in receipt of all appropriate paperwork defining custodial rights of the parents, visitation, and any other conditions important to the district.

This may include notices and announcements sent to separate households, equal access by both parents to grade reporting, and visits to teacher conferences. It is important that all administrators and administrative assistants are aware of the custodial rights of divorced parents. Security guards and school resource officers (SROs) should also be informed of official arrangements, including court orders, pickup, and dismissal procedures.

As superintendent, your office should create a procedure for principals and administrative assistants to keep a list of students whose parents have special arrangements accessible at all times. Most often, a student information system provides a method of posting this as a highlighted advisory so that an individual staff member, reviewing a student's record, is alerted to the prescribed orders. This protocol will ensure that students and families will be served pursuant to judicial agreement.

MCKINNEY-VENTO ACT:[3]
HOMELESS CHILDREN/FAMILIES

The McKinney-Vento Act addresses situations that "homeless" youth face with regard to enrolling, attending, and being successful in school district settings. McKinney-Vento directs local districts to ensure that a homeless child is guaranteed equal access to the same free, appropriate, public education (FAPE) as available to all other children. The tenets of the act are not solely dedicated to adolescents who are "living on the streets." Rather, the act defines "homeless" as individual students who are absent of a fixed, regular, and adequate nighttime residence. Loosely defined, this definition includes students who:

- live with other individuals due to loss of house or apartment or economic hardship;
- reside in hotels or motels, trailers, and so on as alternative accommodations;
- are assigned to shelters or are awaiting foster care placement; or
- sleep in cars, parks, public spaces, squatting in abandoned buildings, substandard housing, bus or train stations, or similar settings.[4]

Homeless youth are entitled to the same educational and ancillary services afforded to other students to help them meet the academic achievement and assessment standards to which all students are held,[5] meaning that students within this category are not to be separated from the regular school district climate, culture, and environment. They are scheduled to take a regular course load, and they are able to enjoy the same extracurricular benefits as other students in the district.

Originally authored in 1987 under Title VII-B of the McKinney-Vento Homeless Assistance Act (42 USC 11431 et seq.) (McKinney-Vento Act), the act was reauthorized by the No Child Left Behind (NCLB) Act of 2001. The verbiage dictates that a student, who is considered "homeless" based on the aforementioned criteria, must be registered in the district of her last permanent residence. In other words, if Mary lives in Town A and her parents lose their apartment and move to Town B to stay in the basement of a relative, Mary still remains in Town A for a period of time. However, Mary's parents can also choose to register in Town B if they are living legally in the residence and can provide an affidavit of landlord (or comparable district-specific documentation) to prove where Mary is currently domiciled. The "home" district also provides transportation for the student to and from school.

Specific considerations were added to the act after it was reauthorized under NCLB, and these conditions have now become a permanent part of the educational landscape. Such changes and considerations include:

- prohibitions against segregating homeless students (removal of separate programs);
- requirement for transportation to and from school of origin;
- immediate school enrollment requirement (if there is a dispute over school placement, the district where enrollment is desired must register the student pending the resolution of the dispute);

- determination for school placement that should be in the best interest of the student (e.g., keep student in the district of the last permanent residence unless requested by the parents or guardians); and
- appointment of a homeless liaison in all school districts.[6]

Superintendents must take an active role in the registration and formal education of those students who are considered homeless under McKinney-Vento. Some districts will have more cases than others based on socioeconomic considerations and other climate conditions of the town or city. Domicile investigation officers and/or the district registrar should work with the family and student to ensure proper registration and program implementation are occurring. Periodic audits of the residency of the student will help ensure that the student is enrolled properly for future school years and program considerations.

SUMMARY AND FUTURE CONSIDERATIONS

It is important to remember that students are the responsibility of the CSA from the minute they enter the district on any given school day to the minute they leave for dismissal. The mission only "works" if parents and community stakeholders feel a sense of comfort in the administration's ability to lead and manage a district effectively as well as provide a safe and educational learning environment for all students.

Let's face it—parents want a better life than they had for their children. Students are faced with issues in their young adult lives where they will seek assistance from the only safe haven they know and those individuals running the "show." Some students will see teachers and administrators more during a day than their own parents. This is a systematic change to education as a whole, where households are seeing both parents working several jobs and even the students are working as well.

In addition, consider the following in family law and policy:

- What other programs can be established to assist families in need in your district?
- Make sure that students with divorced parents, who have specific orders or guardianship instructions, have electronic notes/documents on file for quick reference for front-office staff.
- Accommodate divorced parents, with joint custody, on informational items being sent home to both residences.
- Those students and families considered "homeless" are usually going through a temporary hardship that will hopefully rectify itself within several months. However, be assured that students under the McKinney-Bento

Act aren't domiciled in a neighboring district for athletic advantage. As an example, a student lives in your district with an aunt because he is considered "homeless" because his mother was evicted from her apartment. Under the act, he has the right to stay in his original district based on the hardship. You may find that his new permanent residence will be with the aunt (which makes that address his new domicile) and that he is continuing at his original district because they need him to complete the soccer season.

Chapter 6

Mental Health Law and Children

Never give up on someone with a mental illness. When "I" is replaced by "We," illness becomes wellness.

—Shannon L. Alder

Mental health laws are those laws and statutes relating to the rights and treatment of persons with mental illness or a developmental disability, with a special emphasis on Section 504 and Individuals with Disabilities Education Act (IDEA). These laws greatly impact nearly every aspect of the school district (e.g., staffing, budget, accommodations, physical space) and, in turn, the role of the superintendent of schools. Protocols and procedures subsequent to these laws include student evaluations; Intervention and Referral Services (I&RS); confidentiality of mental, special education, and health records; and litigation considerations. Undiagnosed mental health issues in students greatly affect school districts as a whole, district budgets, and the role of the administration.

Educators often feel heightened anxiety and helpless when faced with the mental health needs of their students.[1] Mental illness can be defined as a health condition that changes a person's thinking, feelings, or behavior (or all three) that causes the person distress and difficulty in functioning.[2] A critical gap exists between those who need mental health services and those who receive mental health services.[3]

The latest available data estimates 15 million children in the United States have a diagnosable mental health or a behavioral disorder; however, less than one-third of these individual children receive the necessary treatment and behavioral interventions needed to solve their mental health problems.[4] Of these students, 11 percent demonstrated a significant impairment, with 5 percent having an "extreme functional" impairment. Of that number, only

71

20 percent of these students received any mental health interventions in schools.[5]

The National Alliance on Mental Illness indicates that adolescents have diagnosable mental disorders that range from attention-deficit/hyperactivity disorder to autism to chronic behavioral issues, while a small percentage (8 percent) of these students meet the criteria for major depression.[6]

School is arguably the best place for educators and students to become increasingly aware of mental health problems and mental disorders.[7] If school districts would conduct schoolwide screenings, mental health issues could be "caught" and treated early. Teachers, counselors, and staff, who would identify at-risk students to be sent for further evaluation, would complete these screenings.[8]

The research on brain development and learning emphasizes that students cannot perform to their potential, in consideration of academic achievement, without attention to their mental health needs. The most successful districts include schools that incorporate mental health knowledge and intervention methods to assist students in need, whereas districts that are completely void in addressing mental health issues will still deal with "indirect costs" associated with principal's office visit, utilization of a one-to-one aide, and other interventions that would have been more successful if the individual student was receiving mental health services.

Districts are beginning to add "Drop-In" centers to counseling programs where students can meet discretely with counselors and social workers, without reservation or scheduled appointment, to discuss serious concerns or adolescent issues involving family, friends, and themselves.

Students who receive some scheduled mental health interventions have a reduced rate of course failures, dropout rate, and referrals to special education.[9] Specific mental health interventions address effects on entire school populations and work to enhance positive school environments. Relevant research clearly demonstrates that in-school mental health programs, interventions, and related services benefit students, teachers, and the school district as a whole by:

- increasing student attendance;
- enhancing academic performance;
- growing higher graduation rates;
- improving student behavior;
- creating positive school climates; and
- retaining teachers.[10]

Most often, district personnel depend on counselors to handle most student crisis situations, including mental health issues. School counseling has taken more of an academic role over the past several decades in consideration of increased assessments and greater access for students to postsecondary institutions. The average workload for a school counselor does not allow for enough time to identify and work with students who are suffering from a mental health crisis.

The American School Counselor Association recommends a 250 student per counselor ratio, but the latest reported data (2008–2009) records the average ratio as 457:1. Five states—Louisiana (238:1), Mississippi (234:1), New Hampshire (233:1), Vermont (207:1), and Wyoming (197:1)—were operating at or above that recommended level. California had the largest gap with 814 students per counselor.[11] As evidenced, assistance in this area is scarce, and a limited number of trained personnel are available to assist with mental health issues surrounding students.

School districts need to provide the necessary space and access to healthcare professionals to assist in helping to identify students in need and implement programs that will make students with mental health concerns successful in a regular setting. Budgetary considerations must include appropriate staff to handle these specific issues. This includes fully staffed child study teams and additional school psychologists assigned to individual school buildings. Most faculty and staff members are not trained to identify and provide modifications for students with mental health needs.

School psychologists have the unique training and qualifications that would permit students to be evaluated and "seen" during a school day when immediate attention to a situation is needed. They ensure that mental health services are infused into instruction that benefits the child academically and socially.[12]

With the appropriate resources, school psychologists can assist the superintendent in providing counseling services; implementing schoolwide prevention programs; consulting with teachers to help them meet the academic, behavioral, and mental health needs of students; conducting suicide and crisis assessments; collecting data on students to make informed programmatic and behavioral modification decisions; acting as a liaison to community service providers; and working with families.[13] In all, assisting students with undiagnosed mental issues during a school day by addressing individual concerns enhances the school environment and overall productivity of the district.

SUMMARY AND FUTURE CONSIDERATIONS

Many children are faced with mental health issues, and many more live with parents who live each day with mental health burdens. One can make a good argument that school districts need more psychologists and counselors than classroom teachers in preparing students for both academic success and social awareness. Without mental stability, students will not have an ability to concentrate and advance in their studies. Further burdens will be placed on the district creating an atmosphere of dismal reproach, stopping the district mission of preparing twenty-first-century leaders.

In addition, consider the following in mental health law and children:

- Should mental health and behavioral screenings take place for students and as early as the primary grades?
- The role of the school counselor has become more academic in nature over the past several decades. What can be done to ensure that counselors spend more time on social issues with students and peers rather than mostly schedules, classes, and standardized assessments?

Chapter 7

Children's Health Law and Policy

He who has health has hope; and he who has hope has everything.

—Arabic proverb

This section relates the office of the superintendent to the purpose and basic principles of public health, including health promotion, disease prevention, and health protection. Case studies and research in the areas of obesity, reproductive health rights of minors, mandatory school immunizations, student drug testing, and violence prevention are just some ways that a superintendent illustrates the application of "public health jurisprudence" from the national to the state levels and ultimately into the classrooms.

LIFE-THREATENING FOOD ALLERGIES

In 2013, the Centers for Disease Control & Prevention (CDC) published the first national comprehensive guidelines for school food allergy management created to protect the physical and emotional health of students with food allergies. These guidelines provide information and strategies for districts and define federal laws and regulations with regard to student allergies and school systems.

School district administrators and healthcare professionals must be aware of those students who suffer from reactions to specific food allergens and insist on an individual management plan to ensure that these individual students are safe within their schools. Some plans incorporate an EpiPen to be utilized in an emergency situation to help save a student's life. District school officials, at times, create a plan that includes an allergen "free" table (e.g., nut-free table), classroom, or even entire school building in order to make the school environment a safe haven for those individuals with severe food allergies.

Life-threatening allergies have greatly affected the landscape of education in consideration of cafeterias and food service providers, school lunches and snacks for students, regulations for serving homemade cupcakes and "treats" for classroom birthday celebrations, and educating parents on important public health issues.

A district superintendent is tasked with the responsibility to set in motion a plan to ensure that all constituent groups are aware of the dangers of specific allergies to students and what steps the district has taken to ensure the health and safety of all individuals. The superintendent must do the following:

- Lead the school district's coordinated approach to manage food allergies by promoting, disseminating, and communicating food allergy–related policies to all faculty, staff, families, and the community. She must be familiar with federal and state laws, including regulations and policies relevant to the obligations of schools to students with food allergies and ensure that each school has a "team" that is responsible for food allergy management.
- Prepare for food allergy emergencies by ensuring that responses to life-threatening food allergy reactions are part of the school district's approach to emergency planning and procedures. Periodic "code blue" drills must be implemented and practiced on a regular basis.
- Assure that administrators, faculty, and staff are trained in EpiPen utilization and receive professional development on the effects of student reactions to food allergies and how to respond in those situations.
- Educate students and school community members in order to raise awareness about food allergies by incorporating considerations regarding prevention and reaction to allergies in the district curriculum and in communications sent home and posted on school websites.
- Create and maintain a healthy and safe school environment by increasing awareness of food allergies and enforcing policies that prohibit discrimination and bullying against students with food allergies.[1]

IMMUNIZATIONS

The CDC argues that school vaccination protocols are part of the top ten public health achievements of the twentieth century.[2] School immunizations are an important safety and regulatory issue for the school district and superintendent. In order to prevent the school community from the spread of certain communicable diseases, boards of education require the immunization of pupils against certain diseases in accordance with state statutes.

Several national studies concluded that states, with schools that had requirements for vaccinations, had lower incidences of mumps and measles when enforcement of the policies included the exclusion of unvaccinated students from school.[3] States with school vaccination laws require children at an appropriate age to be vaccinated for several communicable diseases (e.g., varicella, mumps, measles).

Although the laws are subject to individual medical, religious, and philosophical exceptions, most mandate that children be vaccinated before entering a school district. Failure to attain the appropriate vaccinations can result in a student being denied entry from school. School vaccination laws have been challenged by parents and other "anti-vaccinationists"[4] on legal, social, and medical grounds, where some parents fear harmful effects from the introduction of foreign particles into the human body. The legal challenges to vaccination protocols include:

- contradicting claims of the constitutional principles of individual liberty and due process;
- unnecessary governmental interference with an individual and his ability to decide about his own health; and
- infringing on the religious traditions and beliefs under the First Amendment to the Constitution.[5]

Government offices and procedural guidelines are not what "encourages" any person to be vaccinated; rather, "strong incentives" (e.g., ability to attend school) cause parents to actively seek compliance on vaccination conditions. *Hazen v. Strong*[6] was the first case in very early U.S. history to engage in this debate, where the Vermont Supreme Court upheld the right for a local town council to pay for the vaccination of citizens exposed to smallpox even though there were no reported cases in the community.

As seen in the *Hazen* decision, judges traditionally aligned themselves with legislators, school board administrators and trustees, and public health individuals who stressed vaccinations for community well-being. Vaccination laws in schools serve as a "safety net" for unvaccinated children who would otherwise be placed in a school environment where their risks of spreading and contracting disease are heightened.

Enough research and evidence exists that vaccination requirements for child care institutions and schools improve vaccination coverage and reduce rates of communicable diseases.[7] However, many contemporary arguments against school vaccination laws resemble those of anti-vaccinationists from the past. Parents and advocates are still skeptical about the safety and side effects of vaccines, the need for vaccines, government interference, and conflicts with religious beliefs. These concerns continue to receive legislative attention and litigation as parents challenge the laws governing entrance into schools and vaccinations.[8]

The superintendent is responsible to ensure that all district policies meet federal and state guidelines[9] pertaining to vaccinations. Consulting with a district's local health department officials and board attorney as well as ensuring that all protocols are correctly in place and meet all requirements is an appropriate immediate step for any superintendent just entering the position. The superintendent is also charged with handling objections to vaccinations from parents based on exemption criteria or any vaccination that may be medically contraindicated.[10]

For immunizations that are contraindicated, a written statement from any physician licensed to practice medicine or an advanced practice nurse indicating that an immunization is medically contraindicated for a specific period of time and the reasons for the medical contraindication may exempt a pupil from the specific immunization for the period of time specified in the statement. An example of this exemption includes those students who may be allergic to the chemical composition of a vaccine.

A student may also be exempted from a required immunization if his parent submits a signed statement explaining how the actual administration of the immunizing agent conflicts with the student's religious beliefs or practices. A general philosophical or even a moral objection to immunizations is not considered an acceptable reason to exempt a student on religious grounds. Any student exempt due to medical or religious considerations may be temporarily excused from school by the superintendent during a vaccine-preventable disease outbreak (or threat of an outbreak), as determined by a state health representative.

Court-Related Case Summary: Immunizations

U.S. Court of Appeals, Second Circuit

Nicole Phillips, individually and on behalf of B.P. and S.P., minors, Dina Check, on behalf of minor M.C., Fabian Mendoza—Vaca, individually and on behalf of M.M. and V.M., minors, Plaintiffs—Appellants, v. City of New York, Eric T. Schneiderman, in his official capacity as Attorney General, State of New York, Dr. Nirav R. Shah, in his official capacity as Commissioner, New York State Department of Health, New York City Department of Education, Defendants—Appellees. (Docket No. 14–2156—cv)

In New York State, plaintiffs challenged a requirement that all students be vaccinated in order to attend the public schools, based on constitutional grounds. The plaintiffs argued that the vaccination requirement by statute, which is subject to medical and religious types of exemptions, violated due process, the Free Exercise Clause of the First Amendment, the Equal Protection Clause of the Fourteenth Amendment, the Ninth Amendment, and both state and municipal law. Plaintiffs also argued that a state regulation permitting school authorities to temporarily exclude students who are exempted from the vaccination requirements during an "outbreak" of sorts is unconstitutional. The defendants (City of New York et al.) moved to dismiss the cause, and the court granted the motion. On appeal the decision was upheld. The court reasoned that the statute and regulation are a constitutionally permissible exercise of the state's "police power" and do not infringe on any free exercise of religion.

SUMMARY AND FUTURE CONSIDERATIONS

School district regulations and children's health are an integral partnership in justifying the preparation and standards set for all students in connection with the goals established by the individual school district, mandates on student achievement, and overall wellness. Chief school administrators are charged with establishing and following the policies and laws that are put in place to protect students, teachers, and other personnel from health concerns, allergies, and other specific health-related issues. A strong and positive working relationship with the district medical team and lead administrators in pupil personnel services is an absolute necessity when ensuring that a healthy school community is established in the district.

Also consider the following in children's health law and policy:

• What steps would you take if you received an immunization exemption letter based on religion?
• Parents must be reminded that wellness checks should occur during specific developmental stages of childhood development.

Chapter 8

Resources for Child Assistance

People don't care how much you know, until they know how much you care.

—Theodore Roosevelt

TRAGEDY

It is devastating and unfortunate; however, a superintendent will inevitably at one time during her career as an administrator have to handle the fallout from a tragedy that has occurred in the district. This includes the death of a student due to illness, accident, or other injury. The chief school administrator (CSA) must follow certain steps with regard to incidents in consideration of protecting and providing help for students and staff and ensuring that the incident is handled in a sensitive, confidential, and caring manner. Here are some considerations for a CSA during these types of crises:

1. Scheduled work and appointments for that day are put on hold. Cancel meetings, evaluations, lunch—whatever is on the calendar is now to be removed. The superintendent must physically be on site (at the building the student attended) at the start of the day to show that she is there to assist students, faculty, and families in their greatest time of need.
2. If the board doesn't already know, they must be informed immediately. A personal phone call is best when delivering news of this tenor.
3. The superintendent should contact the board attorney or public information officer and have a statement prepared and ready to be read or submitted should the tragedy be covered in local news. It is important that a statement is prepared and that statement is followed as outlined by the attorney so as not to divulge any information that would violate any

protections or privacy laws for the family or hinder any investigations by local authorities.

4. Contact must be made to mental health organizations and counselors from surrounding towns to assist with the needs of the student body and counseling that may be necessary on a large-scale basis.

5. The director of pupil personnel services, student assistance counselor, principal, or director of guidance or counseling services should establish "safe rooms" where students can go to discuss feelings and grieve with friends.

6. The counselors and mental health professionals must be left to do their jobs. There are many activities to consider when addressing students with tragedy, especially in consideration of the death of a peer.

7. Food should be made available (possibly donated by a local restaurant or district food service vendor). Food is comfort, so providing this for students and staff is always a plus.

8. Faculty and staff, who are very distraught and too emotional to teach, should have the ability to go home for the day on a "therapeutic leave." A follow-up call with them can occur later in the day; however, as the staff is dealing with students in crisis, an overly emotional proctor or classroom facilitator may hinder their progress. The individual staff member can process what has occurred at home with his own support group.

9. Staff and students, who want to pay their respects at services, must be afforded the opportunity to attend those services. The superintendent should consider providing transportation as warranted should a large portion of the student or staff population wish to attend and request that proper parental permission be obtained for each student.

10. It is overwhelmingly imperative that the superintendent makes sure to debrief with counselors with regard to how they are handling the tragedy as well. School administrators during the Columbine shooting, and more specifically 9/11, neglected to think about themselves—about their own team and how each member was reacting to the tragic events that occurred. It is important to digress and lean on one another before leaving for the day. The crisis team has taken the appropriate steps and measures to ensure the students and faculty were serviced that day, and they helped everyone get through the initial distress of the loss of life. It is the superintendent and her team's turn to seek some assistance for the dialogue and discussions that day.

These are only some of the points to consider when tragedy hits a school district. A superintendent will be judged on how she handled the emotional needs of the district and community in arguably one of its direst times of need. The CSA needs to make herself visible and available to students, faculty, staff, parents, and community members who may have questions with regard to such an event and what steps will be taken moving forward. Handling a situation like this is not only what's right for the students, but it also proves that the superintendent has the knowledge and the leadership to be an important member of the district and entire community.

MENTAL HEALTH ORGANIZATIONS

Partnering with local service organizations, mental health programs, and hospitals will provide adequate and qualified assistance when employees or students are at risk for mental health issues or a tragedy occurs in district. A point person for these individual organizations, most likely in the cabinet (i.e., pupil personnel services director), should act as liaison when help is needed or an issue is at hand. It is also viable to include these organizations in local professional development for school personnel and mental health programs for the student population. As mental health considerations exponentially grow in district and matters of depression, suicide, bullying, dating violence, and LGBTQ become a major part of the school day, districts must "reach out" and create trustful, working relationships with mental health professionals and organizations invested in the community.

SUMMARY AND FUTURE CONSIDERATIONS

No superintendent can do this alone! A CSA must build a network of mental health officials and local organizations to help get through the difficult times along with regular interventions throughout the school year. It's not so much the question "if" something will happen during a superintendent's time in district but rather "when" something will happen in the district. When that time arrives, teams of teachers, administrators, students, parents, and the community stakeholders will be looking to the superintendent to lead and guide them into "safety," returning to them some sense of normalcy and a resilience based on the credo that great leaders know when to truly lead. In times of crisis and tragedy, your leadership and humanity must be decisive and sustainable to ensure that every colleague and student have the assistance needed to move forward.

Also, consider the following with regard to resources for child assistance:

- Don't hesitate to ask for assistance from colleagues and support groups or organizations immediately after a tragedy or crisis occurs.
- Create a community outreach program to foster partnerships with local and national public health and nonprofit organizations.
- Be sure to debrief teams after a crisis. Ensure a colleague or an assistant is tasked with debriefing the superintendent as well.

Chapter 9

Writing Correspondence and Future Legal Considerations

Either write something worth reading or do something worth writing.

—Benjamin Franklin

It is inevitable that a superintendent will find herself in a situation throughout the school year where she will need to draft a response to an incident or make a formal statement with regard to something that has occurred in her district. Today, anything and everything written becomes an immediate and permanent electronic footprint within the world of social media. Although there are certain specific instances where the board attorney will draft letters for/from the superintendent of schools, there are day-to-day memorandums that should have a succinct, legal tone as they are drafted to staff members, parents, and community members. The chief school administrator (CSA) should not hesitate to have the board attorney review any letter being disseminated to the public or individual parents, especially if it contains sensitive information.

BE DIRECT

An official correspondence from a superintendent of schools must be written in the same vein as any document that can and will wind up on a court exhibit list. A superintendent must ensure that the writing contains the correct dates and times of/for the prescribed content; appropriate name spellings; and very specific details with regard to timelines, actions, recommendations, and outcomes.

Statements made by students and staff should be quoted exactly as stated. This includes derogatory terms, "curses," and statements with a sexual connotation.

In other words, a formal response or memorialization must not be "sugarcoated" to attenuate the actions and words of the party, which is the subject of the written correspondence.

It is extremely beneficial to design any correspondence as an outline of examples that support findings and any "past practice" issues that may have occurred in the district relative to the topic at hand in the past, especially if something occurred prior to the superintendent's arrival in district. Further, the correspondence should also reference and even include excerpts from district policy, regulations, and state statutes that are related to the situation at hand. Most important, the writing must be direct when including these reference materials as background to the problem statement and how the situation was handled.

BE TIMELY

Any correspondence that is written must "get" to constituent groups in a timely manner. In the age of social media, this is almost immediate. How quickly the superintendent replies to a situation can make a great difference in the way a situation is contained and how rumors, exaggerated stories, or just misinformation is kept from exponentially growing throughout a school district and the surrounding community.

Incidents that include suspicious persons/vehicles, student misconduct at public events, health issues (communicable disease outbreaks, lice, etc.), perceived and actual threats to student safety, and responses to stories reported in local newsfeeds should be disseminated to constituents in an immediate fashion. Other situations, such as new program initiatives, upcoming events, and announcements, can be forwarded to parents, students, and others with an appropriate lead time.

WRITE TO THE AUDIENCE

A basic rule of writing, but authors at times seem to disregard it, is to identify "who" their audience is. The easy trick is to think about the letter as if it was being read to a room filled with those individuals who will be receiving it. Thus, if one was writing to a room of nuclear physicists, his diction and jargon would be different than if he was addressing parents of kindergarten students. Regardless, a superintendent must ensure that the writing is "to-the-point," and it can also be clearly understood by whoever is reading it. This means that certain terms may have to be defined or a step-by-step procedure or protocol for actions that need to occur may need to be provided.

BE REASSURING

When creating a document for parents and stakeholders, it is imperative that the recipients know that the superintendent has their best interests in mind and is in control of the situation at hand. This is of a heightened expectation in consideration of a school safety event (e.g., lockdown, suspicious person). The tone of the correspondence must be reassuring, in that the intended audience is in support of the way in which the situation was resolved, they are confident that all children are safe, and that the perceived threat or emergency will not continue moving forward. Using different social media vehicles can also help spread a positive, reassuring message. However, a superintendent must be reminded that whatever she disseminates may ultimately appear on a local news broadcast, be printed in the newspaper, and, most important, will become a digital footprint of how she handled this particular occurrence in consideration of future job considerations and interview references.

One final measure a superintendent can take in reassuring a community that a threat or emergency has been "handled" is to disseminate the notices in other languages that are spoken at home in the district. Any large population of parents or community members, where English is not their native language, should be given consideration for information of this magnitude to be translated and sent accordingly. It is the duty of the CSA to ensure that the constituent and stakeholder base is kept apprised of any situation that has affected the school community. Breaking down the language barrier is an added measure in securing support for administrative actions and moving past what has occurred.

LOCAL AUTHORITIES, BODIES, ORGANIZATIONS

Partnering with local nonprofit organizations, community impact groups, and government agencies is an important asset to a paradigm of community engagement that will lead to growing a positive message about the superintendent and the mission that has been established for the district. At times, these organizations can come to the district's aid in consideration of assistance needed with community service, student discipline, legal matters, community perception, and the enhancement of a positive climate in and around the district.

Formulating a partnership agreement with these organizations allows your students, personnel, and partners to become actively involved in the joint programs and public relations benefits that come with each individual partnership. From a legal standpoint, it is extremely important that a superintendent consult with his board attorney on approving an agreement with the partner organization and a resolution by the board (board action), which outlines the extent of the district's partnership with the outside organization and how students and other school community members can or will be involved with that organization. Moving forward, the superintendent must also ensure that students, volunteering to work with these partner agencies, have submitted the appropriate parental permission forms, and workers in these organizations have completed appropriate background or criminal checks to be working with students.

It is further recommended that strict protocols be put in place for those teachers and administrators who are leading these volunteer efforts with regard to supervising students and assuring they are not left alone with workers or individuals outside the district. It is equally important as a community outreach program grows exponentially that a director be placed in charge of its full operation, especially due to the fact that students will be "working" in an out-of-district capacity. Further, as these types of outreach programs can be an excellent way to spotlight a district and its students as well as bring attention to a superintendent's ability as a leader to bridge gaps between community groups and advance student–community engagement and citizenship, one "unfortunate" situation can have an extremely negative impact on both the superintendent and the district and hurt the perception the community and surrounding communities have on the students, teachers, and schools.

PROVIDE RESOURCES (WEBSITES)

In any correspondence to parents, personnel, or community stakeholder groups, resources should always be provided (e.g., websites, addresses, phone numbers) for individuals to find further information and research on a particular topic that is being addressed within a correspondence. Each correspondence sent should indicate that additional information or answers to questions or concerns could be directed to a building principal, director, or the superintendent. It is imperative that individuals, who are receiving information about an incident, event, or emergency, have the ability to continue the conversation or have a point of reference after they read the letter.

This is a very important consideration because unanswered questions from individuals lead to outside discussions, rumors, and the "telephone" game where sometimes a nonincident becomes more of an issue since it wasn't handled correctly.

Individuals who need more answers after reading a district statement need an outlet to continue the conversation. Offer the superintendent website e-mail and other options to accommodate any concerns. When writing an academic correspondence to administrators, staff, and others, be sure to use appropriate grammar, spelling, and citations to identify any research used to reiterate a topic or program. It is customary at a superintendent's advanced degree level to cite using the American Psychological Association (APA) standards in consideration of endnotes and in-text citations.

PROVIDE LEGAL RESEARCH/POLICIES

Whenever correspondence to parents or personnel includes some type of warranted discipline or other measures that need to be taken due to an event or infraction, it is necessary to cite specific areas of state or federal statutes and district policies to reiterate reasons for the action being taken or recommended.

At times, it is also customary to include a copy of said policies and statutes for the other parties' perusal and information. Remember that every correspondence should be written in the same manner it would be written if it would appear on a court document. The more evidence provided, at the time you are sending the letter, with regard to why the record was created will only help support the case being made if it should reach a higher authority. Hence, the more "black-and-white" the issue appears as being an infraction or misrepresentation of some policy or law, the more justified in bringing the matter to the forefront.

LANGUAGES

As mentioned earlier, an important vehicle to utilize when considering the delivery of information to constituents and community groups is to create and disseminate letters and documents in common native languages spoken in district. If there is a medium to large language group in the community, ensure that the information recreated is in those languages so that the information reaches and is understood by a large base of supporters and the actual message is understood.

SPELLING/GRAMMAR CHECK

Who or whom? Them versus him or her? Quotations always cover punctuation marks. As perception is an important consideration of the office, utilization of the written English language including, but not limited to, diction, spelling, and grammar can and will make a major impression on the community—good or bad. The chief education officer is held to the highest academic standard throughout the entire district. Both he and his "office" must model the mission of the district and set an example that exemplifies an accountability and leadership that is an expectation of all personnel and students.

Sending out a correspondence with spelling and grammatical errors, unpresentable letterhead, and an unclear message gives the reader an impression that these things aren't important to the superintendent. The question then becomes, "Well, if the superintendent doesn't care about it, then what's happening in the classrooms?" Besides spell-check and other remedies, a CSA should ensure that an assistant (other than the assistant who may have typed the correspondence) reads through the document carefully to help assist him in perfecting a letter or an announcement.

ATTORNEY REVIEW

As it has been consistently reiterated throughout this handbook (and really cannot be stressed enough), a superintendent or CSA should seek the advice of an attorney on district issues involving personnel, students, and so forth; when she needs reassurance that she has handled a situation properly; or needs assistance with regard to other measures that should be taken and the legal ramifications of such actions or lack thereof. This also holds true for any written correspondence that contains legal and policy issues, especially for a correspondence that a superintendent will be disseminating to the public. Not only is this an important step to follow to protect the very interests of the superintendent but a consideration for the board as well.

SUMMARY AND FUTURE CONSIDERATIONS

As we continue to stress the importance of positive perception in the office of the superintendent, arguably the most important tenet relates to written correspondence and communication with stakeholders. It is important that letters and memorandums sent to parents, officials, and so forth include appropriate references and researched directives as an assurance that what you are disseminating includes meaningful and accurate information. Partnering with community and national organizations is a good way to spread the mission of the district and get students involved with the service aspect of your curricular frameworks.

Also, consider the following when writing to and interacting with stakeholders and constituent groups:

- What should be the duties of a liaison or partnership officer who deals directly with these groups to assist with fund-raisers, awareness events, press releases, and so forth?
- What are some of the negative effects of dealing with outside organizations on the local, state, and national levels (e.g., budget, political influences, fairness to all groups)?

Chapter 10

"I Am Not Responsible,
but I Am to Blame"

It is not only for what we do that we are held responsible, but also for what
we do not do.

—Moliere

For many years, the administrator's credo has always been the saying, "I am
not responsible, but I am to blame." There's absolutely no better—and really,
no easier—way to state the inevitable in the position of superintendent of
schools. Every school district is made up of a plethora of moving parts that
affect hundreds, and even thousands in some districts, of students, personnel,
community members, and the like. Each day throughout the district, these
"parts" continuously make decisions that make up an active school day. Some
of these decisions are good for children—and some of these decisions are not.
Some of these decisions will effect a positive change in district, and others
may put the superintendent on the front page of the local newspaper (not for
a good reason) if not remedied properly.

Regardless of the issues she will face, a successful chief accepts that these
situations are ultimately forthcoming and knows how to react to and solve for
any issue that comes her way. It is impossible to prevent every crisis from occurring, so step 1 is to accept that statement as fact. If a new superintendent is an
individual who in his past roles as a department head, principal, supervisor, or
director had an innate ability to manage all areas in consideration of his department or building, his elevation to the chair of superintendent incorporates the
responsibilities for all of those positions—not to mention all other offices—into
one. From food service, custodians, athletics, purchasing, pension, payroll, and
playground to students, staff, curriculum, buildings and grounds, and every other
aspect of the district, all decisions, initiatives, and responsibility lead to his office.

Of course, we have already assumed all of this prior to reaching this part of the handbook. However, there are some specific areas to really be aware of with regard to statutes, laws, and a true sense of what can "sneak up" on a superintendent if not handled properly. Further, it is just as important to know how to react to these issues when the blame does reach central office with no advanced knowledge it was heading that way!

CRISIS PLANS

School crisis plans should be in central office waiting to be reviewed within the first ten days of the new school year. It is crucial that each building principal develops his own plan, and the leadership team doesn't just copy and paste a template sent by central office personnel. The reasoning behind this is simple: the building principal needs to know how to implement every aspect of the plan when an emergency arises. Hence, he needs to be the author of the plan.

A superintendent must review the plans with his compliance officer and/or school safety director so as to confirm that each plan includes specific components that follow local and federal procedures for active shooter, lockdown, fire, and other events and that all plans utilize the same language and terms so that local police and fire agencies can react to any crisis in an efficient and timely manner. He must further ensure that all evacuation areas are kept strictly confidential and include a secondary evacuation site in the event the first site is compromised or unavailable. Evacuation drills must take place within the first thirty days of the school year at each school building to ensure that the school population has practiced the procedures with local authorities and the administration has the ability to adapt the plan as needed.

TEST BREACHES

Breaches with standardized tests need to be reported in an immediate fashion with regard to the protocols provided to the superintendent via a state's department of education agency. If a breach includes the utilization of electronic mail, the school network, or electronic devices, it may be a proactive step to suspend the network traffic until further direction is received from state and testing officials. Test breaches not only have ramifications due to the academic standing of the district but remedies for breaches also can become very costly for a district, which includes local taxpayer revenue.

It is important for a superintendent to document all actions in consideration of the breach and create a timeline as to what occurred before, during, and after the issue was identified. Students and teachers who are involved in a breach should submit to the superintendent a written statement for the investigation and report. In consideration of a local union, a report of this nature is considered a fact-finding "mission" so as to report the breach accurately, and it is not disciplinary in nature. To avoid issues with personnel and breaches, all personnel must receive the appropriate test administration training prior to administering the test.

Prior to the administering of any state and/or standardized test, staff members should be directed to sign an assurance that they have completed the test training, read the training materials, and understand the importance of confidentiality and reporting procedures. Consider informing the board president of the initial investigation and concern using general terms, but do not reveal any information with regard to personnel or students. The investigation may lead to disciplinary measures that may need to be deliberated later by board members.

MANDATORY PROFESSIONAL DEVELOPMENT

Each state department of education mandates specific professional development trainings that must be completed by all school personnel. Although each state differs with regard to which trainings are required, most topics are related to the health and safety of students in consideration of physical, mental, and social well-being. These mandatory trainings must be completed in order for a district and school personnel to stay in compliance with school district regulations and remain in good standing with regard to credentials and licensing. Subjects of mandatory professional development assist in keeping faculty and staff accountable in consideration of specific areas of oversight and may include, but not be limited to, the following:

- suicide prevention/recognition/reporting;
- PEOSH (Public Employees Occupational Safety and Health)/blood-borne pathogens and so forth;
- integration/infusing English language learners;
- child abuse reporting;
- harassment, intimidation, bullying;
- dyslexia;
- individualized education programs;
- AED (Automated External Defibrillator)/CPR (Cardiopulmonary Resuscitation);
- Health Insurance Portability and Accountability Act (HIPAA);
- Family Educational Rights and Privacy Act (FERPA); and
- school safety procedures or protocols.

REPORTING ABUSE

At the start of every new school year, a superintendent must ensure that all personnel are made aware that any suspicion, allegation, or evidence of child abuse toward a student must be reported to a supervisor or building administrator immediately. This could be abuse suffered at the hands of another student or peer, a teacher, parent, family member, and so on. Regardless if the claim is physical or mental in nature, any derogatory act that has occurred against a child must be investigated thoroughly and the appropriate authorities contacted immediately. As a CSA, this is arguably the most imperative form of reporting when discussing the legal responsibilities of the district. To evidence in a clear manner how important this is, a memorandum outlining the procedure should be sent to all district personnel, a section of the faculty or staff handbook should be dedicated to this topic, and it should be part of the opening-day orientation presentation.

NATIONAL COLLEGIATE ATHLETIC ASSOCIATION CLEARINGHOUSE

If you don't really know what this section is, then some additional research is in your near future! A more important question may be if the director of pupil personnel services or guidance director in the school district understands how the Clearinghouse affects student athletes. The National Collegiate Athletic Association (NCAA) Clearinghouse is the organization responsible for determining the academic eligibility of graduating high school seniors to play Division I or Division II amateur sports in college. Student athletes, who are dedicated to continuing to play sports after high school, must successfully complete a certain battery of courses for credits (Carnegie hours) and maintain a specific grade point average, in tandem with an acceptable SAT score based on a sliding scale (higher GPA/lower SAT), in order to be eligible to play in Division I and II athletic programs.

Most often, a regular education program, as approved by the district board of education, includes an appropriate sequencing of courses and amount of credits to move individual students to postsecondary play after graduation. However, at times students, who fail courses and neglect to recover credits either online or in summer schools, can fall short of the Clearinghouse requirements and be deemed ineligible to play. In consideration of Division I and Division II athletics, there is a good possibility that scholarship monies will be attached to admission into those select colleges and universities.

More complicated in consideration of the Clearinghouse is the fact that some high school athletes don't "peak" until Junior Year, and they may not meet the Clearinghouse requirements because they weren't on any coach or counselor's radar prior to that time. Thus, a district may be left with the best female athlete in the student body without enough of the appropriate credits to receive a full scholarship to a Division I college or university. This scholarship can involve a significant amount of monetary compensation and be seen as a legal concern should your team be liable for not representing the student athlete properly.

To combat this and ensure that district athletes are represented in the most efficient manner, training and professional development opportunities in this area must be afforded to high school guidance counselors, principals, and directors. A superintendent may also consider assigning one counselor (or two) to be responsible specifically for all athletic counseling in order to maintain an optimal arrangement and working relationship between the students and their coaches, teachers, and administrators.

CASH

If there is one thing to learn early in administration, it is that cash is not a friend of the school administrator. There is nothing "good" that can stem from cash being collected and "lying around" in a district desk somewhere over a weekend. Indeed, there will inevitably be collections made for fund-raising efforts and the like from students and faculty. Keeping detailed records of all cash received and providing receipts will ensure that missing monies do not enter the office of the superintendent of schools.

A CSA must establish strict protocols to be followed by all administrators and program facilitators or coaches with regard to the collection and deposit of monies. An additional suggestion would be to create a position in district (usually stationed in a K–12 setting at the high school or middle school where, most likely, the most monies are collected) known as coordinator of student accounts who sits as a treasurer of all programs in district. Regardless of who is handling and accounting the cash, policy must dictate and be firmly stated that all cash deposits be made within forty-eight hours of the money being collected.

Further consideration must be made when linking the collection of cash to parent organizations. Nearly all districts have numerous and specific parent organizations to assist the district in providing programs, celebrations, trips, events, and supplemental equipment (e.g., warm-up jerseys provided by the Basketball Parents Association for the boys and girls basketball teams) who work within their own bylaws through the election of an executive board of parent or community volunteers.

On the surface and for the most part, these groups provide that added sense of local pride to student-based activities, and their support will strengthen the extracurricular component of the mission of the district. These groups include PTO, HSA, OPE, Parent Teacher Organization; Home and School Association; Organization of Parents and Educators and other parent-teacher groups, as well as sport and civic associations. Since these organizations are established to govern themselves, the same must hold true with regard to the collection of association funds, accounting practices, and disbursements for expenses and purchases.

The district, and specifically the superintendent and the office, should not become involved in the financial oversight and collection of funds for these organizations. As they are voluntary in nature, there is no true way to hold individuals accountable for dealing with cash collections who have minimal training and/or interest in the accounting principles necessary to run a school district. Further, district policies should outline the district's "relationship" with parent organizations and the procedures that must be followed in obtaining permissions to utilize school sites and so on.

LATE REPORTING (GRANTS, ETC.)

It is important that an executive assistant or an assistant administrator keeps a "tickler" file of all important due dates for grants and reports due to state and federal government agencies. Although all grant writing and grant opportunities are of importance to the district budget in conjunction with offering programs without inflating the local tax levy, the most important grant management revolves around federal Title Grants, No Child Left Behind (NCLB) Act, and Every Student Succeeds Act (ESSA).

Along with the accountability regulations, project plans, and title amendments that go along with securing federal funding for programs, equipment, and services, meeting specific submission and reporting deadlines are imperative to assuring that the appropriate allotment of grant monies is received and can continue to be utilized on a daily basis. Late reporting and missing submission deadlines will negatively impact the grant funding a district can receive for major programs, and, regardless of how small the monetary allotment is, it is extremely difficult to answer the question, posed by a member of the community, "What is the reason behind the district receiving a significant decrease in federal grant aid this year when compared to last year?"

In order to avoid an adverse impact with regard to such an integral fiduciary district necessity, it is customary to appoint an assistant or deputy superintendent or director of grants, research, and development to be the lead person with respect to federal grants management, specific deadlines, and the submission of such important documents.

BOARD POLICY

As stated in an earlier section, the one sure way of providing evidence to a board or constituent group that a superintendent is ineffective in his duties is for the superintendent to be indecisive, unwavering, and irresolute when following board policy. A board of education, and, in turn, a board trustee's whole existence, is to represent a constituent base within a community and create specific policies and regulations to guide the mission of the practice.

The most successful school chiefs utilize strong leadership skills and those adopted board policies and regulations as the guiding force when advancing the mission and enhancing the academic abilities of the students in the district. A successful CSA also knows how and when to recommend changes and updates to policies in consideration of the district, pupils, and personnel where laws and state mandates have been added, amended, or attenuated; the community has required some change in a philosophy based on a community need or interest; and dialogue between different groups agrees that a change in a particular policy would benefit the greater good for a greater cause in the district.

As professionals in the field of educational leadership argue that board policy is considered the Bible in each particular district, it must be respected enough so that the most attention be placed ensuring it is up to date and that your administrative team, faculty, support personnel, and students are aware of the procedures that need to be followed for each particular policy. This is a monumental task; however, putting together a consistent and transparent process will permit a CSA to be as accurate as possible and be the most proactive she can in consideration of any and all situations that come to fruition during any given school day. Assuring that a superintendent is best suited for this task can be accomplished in several ways:

1. Ensure that a board policy committee be established and meet regularly prior to monthly, regular meetings of the board.
2. Consider posting policies online so that they are open to the public and more easily accessible to parents, students, and staff members. It is difficult to argue with someone who didn't follow a particular policy when he couldn't reference the policy prior to or during the infraction or problem taking place.
3. Audit several policies (approximately five to seven) per month for review with the board of education both in committee and for revision during the public portion of a regularly scheduled board meeting. This shows that the superintendent is being proactive in consideration of district guidelines. These policies do not necessarily need to consist of policies that are set to

expire or have not been updated for a long period of time. Rather, these are random policies that are chosen in a monthly audit sequence to assure that all policies are reviewed and reapproved every three to five years.

4. Consider creating a district parliamentarian position who would be the individual administrator or confidential assistant responsible for researching policies when needed and editing those policies that are revised by your board.

5. Utilize an outside consulting firm or attorney for your policy needs. Individual state school board associations also provide services that can answer policy questions and create templates for new policies as needed in the district.

"HEY, HOW LONG HAS THAT MOUND OF SOIL BEEN THERE?"

Guess what? As the superintendent of schools sits in his office under mounds of paperwork, reports, evaluations, and program proposals to consider, there is a pile of dirt or construction materials sitting somewhere in district for the past several years. Of course, he is not responsible for this dirt arriving to the district one cold and stormy April afternoon when the former director of buildings and grounds thought there would be a need to backfill an area of grading that had been completed after the new playground equipment was installed at First Avenue Elementary School. But when Frank Johansen, parent of two young girls running for board of education and a frequent vocal critic of the superintendent at monthly board meetings, decided to take a sample of soil from the pile and have it tested at an independent lab, the results now make the superintendent and trustees responsible!

Be aware of vendors, contractors, and other agents of the board who may leave projects unfinished with certain safety and health hazards outstanding. A superintendent must ensure that her maintenance and grounds personnel are repairing fences and placing appropriate signage in unauthorized areas. Regardless of an incident that occurs, an individual of the legal profession will "poke holes" in the protocols you have in place to keep incidents from occurring. A superintendent can gain favor with the community and her trustees if she has taken nearly every precaution in an attempt to avoid an unthinkable situation.

LEAD AND ASBESTOS AND MOLD, OH MY!

At some point during her tenure as superintendent, a CSA will be faced with one or more environmental issues that, if not handled quickly and efficiently, may lead to public scrutiny, costly remediation, and school closures. It is important that a district contracts with an independent environmental consultant who can assist in creating and administering a proactive schedule of reviewing and assessing all facility areas of the district that are delineated as high-risk areas for environmental hazards and emergencies.

As a consultant works together alongside the district business administrator and director of buildings and grounds or plant engineer to inspect areas including, but not limited to, boilers and HVAC systems, roofing, potable faucets and drinking fountains, basement areas, and floor tiles, the superintendent should direct her team to take proactive steps to mitigate any "fallout" from reports of elevated levels or findings with regard to environmental concerns. In consideration of lead in water, appropriate filters must be placed on all district faucets and test random sites frequently. A superintendent must be familiar with the district AHERA[1] policy or program and verify if identified areas of asbestos had been removed in prior years. Air quality testing in damp areas or areas that had an active leak or flood may also be considered; however, the district must use caution when testing since all data must be reported and some air samples will read high in levels for mold, spores, and so forth in an affected area that may be within an allowable range but will create a perception of an environmental issue, causing an unwarranted alert and hysteria by parents, teachers, and other stakeholders that is neither necessary nor warranted.

AUDITS AND CORRECTIVE ACTIONS

Audits are an effective way to prove that protocols and standard operating procedures with regard to particular systems either meet or surpass a standard proficiency in consideration of personnel, curriculum, fiscal management, and board governance areas. Each district has standard audits that are completed each year and identify weaknesses that need to be modified and remediated. Included in this standard set of audits are the district's Comprehensive Annual Financial Report (CAFR), U.S. Department of Agriculture food service verifications, transportation, and tuitions and services related to students with disabilities. After deficiencies are found in an audit, a corrective action plan (CAP) is designed to remediate the observed infractions and assist district personnel in correcting the identified issue.

An important note to mention is directed to those individual items in an audit that are identified one year to the next and are known as repeat findings. As an auditor has been charged to test internal systems and find deficiencies, one can almost guarantee that some issue will be identified. Although there cannot be an expectation that an audit report will reveal all areas with 100 percent compliance, there can be an expectation of the superintendent's office to remediate all past findings and avoid repeats.

PROTECTING STUDENTS AND HIRING EMPLOYEES

I would venture to guess that there aren't too many (if any) applicants who include a "bad" reference on a résumé or application. With regard to hiring personnel and student advisory positions in district, each individual is recommended to the board by the superintendent, therefore making faculty and staff the superintendent's ultimate responsibility. Where the blame may fall lends itself to those individuals or committees who "screened" applications, conducted preliminary round interviews, and thus made a formal recommendation to the superintendent's office. Law and policy are extremely straightforward when working with a human resources department to hire individuals to work with students.

As it is the top priority to keep students safe, there are several direct factors to consider prior to recommending an employee to hire and work with the greatest commodity in your district—your students:

1. All candidates set for recommendation must have the appropriate teaching or professional certificate (or eligibility) for the position in which they are being hired.
2. Check the candidate's transcripts to verify that degrees have been awarded and match what has been submitted on a résumé and application for truth and accuracy.
3. Work with district health professionals so that the candidate has received proper immunizations and tests.
4. Ensure the candidate is scheduled for and then completes a fingerprint or criminal background check and wellness physical with the school physician.
5. Perform an Internet and media search on all potential recommendations.
6. Call references and the candidate's last place of employment. Consider ending the conversation with the question, "So, if you had the opportunity, would you hire Johnny again in your district?"

This is the most important process in consideration of all of the daily routines of the district's schools chief. No one truly knows how any employee is capable of acting or performing once hired in district, but missing something blatantly obvious to a pre-employment screening process or research will land the blame solely on the office of the superintendent. A central administration or cabinet position such as chief talent officer is an effective way to assure all candidates are vetted thoroughly prior to a final recommendation to your board. It is also imperative that the human resources director stays current on his professional development and any changes relative to employment law and the equal rights of all employees.

SUMMARY AND FUTURE CONSIDERATIONS

It is inevitable that things are going to happen. More important, the successful CSA understands and accepts this to be true and prepares not to prevent what is inevitable but how to react, remediate, and respond to what has occurred. It is important to be as transparent as possible in order to continue to earn the trust of your constituents and stakeholders, and when a mistake is made, at times an apology goes a very long way. The most important aspect of admitting to a mistake is also outlining what steps have been taken so that the mistake is not made again.

Many, if not most, of a district's "issues" do not stem from the superintendent's office; rather, the superintendent is usually the secondary source sent in to "fix" the issue at hand. Issues that arise must be dealt with in an immediate fashion, and successful administrators will anticipate public outcry and what the reaction of parents, students, teachers, and so forth will be based on the decisions made and the actions shown by the superintendent of schools.

In addition, consider the following when dealing with district issues:

- What/Where are the greatest impacts made to the students and the instructional program?
- What other offices (e.g., state comptroller, local authorities, environmental agency, labor relations) should be contacted in consideration of a high-profile situation that has occurred in district?
- What type of board policy should reflect how the superintendent reacts to negative publicity with regard to informing the public and reporting to the board?

Chapter 11

How to Pass a Referendum for Construction Projects

We shape our buildings; thereafter, they shape us.

—Winston Churchill

In consideration of law and protections for the rights of the children for which a superintendent is responsible for on a daily basis, facilities and building maintenance play a major role in assuring that those rights remain preserved. Buildings that are older and poorly maintained prior to a superintendent arriving to the district may have major health and safety violations in consideration of code, federal laws, and local compliance issues that must be remediated.

Although the cleanliness of the building and the perception of a fully operational plant is something that parents and stakeholders witness on building visits and "drive-bys" when trekking to the local supermarket, masking serious repair and construction concerns will one day expire and leave the district in a monetary crisis as major infrastructure systems reach their end of life. These concerns for the welfare of students, faculty, staff, and parents include a wide spectrum of issues from asbestos, lead, and crumbling building facades, heating and ventilation considerations, boilers, alarms and fire suppressant upgrades, access relative to the Americans with Disabilities Act (ADA) to roofing, and water penetration. Even overcrowding becomes a health and safety concern when population density reaches both educational and building occupancy levels that could not be predicted or planned for otherwise.

The idea of "maintaining" buildings, housing necessary and mandated programs, and meeting capacity requirements include a comprehensive plan that, in many districts, loses out when it competes with budget cuts and board decisions to place monies in areas other than facilities in order to meet the needs of district issues related to personnel, instruction and program, extracurricular activities, and other areas of governance. As capital reserves set aside may run deficient or project costs surpass those amounts, the chief school administrator (CSA) will be left with making the recommendation to his board as to which projects take priority over others, what other programs will be sacrificed to secure funds for these facility needs, and how the district will be able to sustain these facilities' projects over multiple years. One consideration is to fund and complete a multitude of necessary projects and ask that the taxpayers of the community fund it as debt service over a period of time. This is what is commonly known as a construction referendum.

A construction referendum is a local district proposal and community vote that affirms or denies a district's request to "bond" for a large amount of money for the purpose of completing specific projects, usually based upon enrollment expansion, technology and program enhancements, and/or student health and safety needs in a particular school district. State departments of education, at times, provide tax relief in the form of debt service aid to those districts voting for referendums in the affirmative, and those aid numbers and percentages are based on a specific formula relative to eligible projects based on a needs assessment submitted by the district to state officials.

Preparing for, submitting, and marketing a referendum vote is an arduous task that can be frustrating throughout the process. In following the steps to advertising and providing information to the public with regard to educating the community on project specifications, costs, and timelines, there are clear parameters to follow and barriers to avoid. However, a positive "vote" and passage for such an important cause can be a fulfilling moment in a superintendent's professional career, and it can further be a testament to his achievements and leadership in the community.

From a legal perspective and in conjunction with most state electioneering laws, a superintendent must take added steps to keep his involvement with any referendum vote to a "neutral" standing. In other words, a superintendent can't tell individuals or parents to vote "for" or "yes" when it comes to the referendum question. This includes any literature disseminated or posted with regard to the referendum projects and question. What a superintendent can do is provide information with regard to the proposal and educate the community with regard to the history of the district and past referendum attempts, a needs assessment and why individual projects need to be completed, the tax impact or loan interest with regard to the projects, expected time frames for project completion, and other information pertinent to the projects and their impact on the community. Consultation with the board attorney in consideration of information, fliers, or literature that the district will be mailing or disseminating to constituent groups and citizens is a definite protocol to be followed.

Although the preparation, timeliness of the vote, advertising campaign, and workload are similar in every instance of a referendum, elections and election outcomes define their own unique phenomena. Transparency and making oneself available to answer questions and meet with constituents throughout the entire process are key elements to building a foundation of trust that can lead to a successful campaign. Further considerations in strengthening this type of a strategic plan include the following eight elements.

1. Political Atmosphere

A referendum that includes an impact to the local tax levy, no matter how small the impact, will not be overwhelmingly popular with taxpayers and local government officials. In order to move forward with project considerations, a superintendent must first receive approval and direction from a majority of the board trustees. As this inevitably is "half the battle" won in consideration of elected or appointed officials within the local government, the other half (municipal side) may not be as easy to convince or garner enough support.

Scheduling a private work meeting to discuss proposed projects and expenses is the formidable way to provide officials with plans for a referendum of this nature. This meeting should be offered well in advance of any official announcement, with regard to project plans, provided to the rest of the community. This supports that the superintendent is looking to engage the entire community leadership in anticipation of feedback and input into the proposal. There should be no surprise that a meeting of this nature is poorly attended, or if it doesn't happen at all. In many political arenas, support of tax increases for projects and programs outside the normal scope of annual budget considerations can be toxic for elected members of government especially if their term is expiring and they must consider "running" for reelection in the upcoming election cycle.

Offering the meeting and inviting those officials to be a part of the process from the beginning are the only responsibilities the superintendent has in attempting to get all government bodies together for this important venture. At times, when each township or city is different and unique in its own setting, officials will show support of the endeavor in the only way they truly can—by not speaking out against it publicly to their base. Although those individuals may not exactly place a sign on their lawn in support of the project, a discreet absence with respect to any antireferendum campaign is a hidden vote of confidence for your side.

2. Hiring a Consultant

Referendums can be costly, and prereferendum expenses can add up quickly. These early expenses can also be dangerous if a referendum doesn't pass and local monies used can never be recouped. Nonetheless, a referendum consultant can be an integral part of your team in consideration of marketing and strategy with respect to voter awareness and turnout.

Parent Meetings

It is important to educate and inform all community members with regard to the referendum question you have established; however, strategy may dictate that those particular groups of which you are most responsible (and will show their direct support of the project) should receive the most attention. The ultimate group meeting this definition is parents.

Scheduling meetings with district parent groups to present the project, plans, and tax impact will assure that the message is reaching the right constituents since they have the most to gain from the referendum passing in the affirmative. Parents are also the best networking device since they can act as tendrils with respect to getting the superintendent's message out to other parents and supporters. Those parents who support the cause are the best advocates and have a vested interest in seeing that the proposal gets enough votes to be successful.

Q & A With Legal Counsel, Bond Counsel, and Architects

With any construction referendum, or construction or capital project for that matter, it is in the best interest of the administrative team to enhance the transparency of the proposal by answering questions for parents and township citizens at nighttime meetings and other board venues. It's simple—if professionals like architects and bond counsel want to be compensated for the project, they will help you "sell it" to the constituent base. Bond counsel can be considered the most important entity of the team for taxpayer purposes because everyone wants to know how any capital project, outside the scope of the regular budget parameters, will affect their pocketbook. A superintendent must ensure that there are enough handouts and presentation literature available for individuals present and that the presentation is videoed and posted with materials to the district website.

Literature

As stated in the beginning of the chapter, the superintendent and administration cannot tell voters to vote "yes"; however, anyone can remind voters to get out and vote. The literature designed and ultimately disseminated must be factual and informational in nature. Public relations personnel or teams must take care to stay away from "flashy" print and glossy paper so as to avoid the public perception that the district has money to spend on election materials while the board keeps asking for more money to operate. Providing pictures and drawings to inform stakeholders about the projects they will be voting on during election day is necessary and beneficial to the process, along with including the date and polling times for the election as well.

3. Follow Board Policies on Electioneering

Although there are state and federal laws with regard to the "do's" and "don'ts" of elections, some boards adopt electioneering policies with regard to what can be done on campus by personnel in consideration of national and state elections as well as the local school board elections and special questions (referendum). It is important that the policies are in place and well known to members of district staff and the board as well to avoid any confrontation or formal complaint prior to, during, or after the election takes place.

4. Meet with Special Interest Groups

It is essential that the superintendent is not biased when disseminating information out to the public with regard to a referendum question. There may be specific public groups that the superintendent and trustees may wish to meet with more often due to their accessibility and interest in the projects. As an example, parent groups in schools have the most concerns about construction projects since their children are those individual citizens who will be directly affected by the projects and reap the benefits after the projects are completed. Speaking to these groups for which a superintendent has an open-ended meeting invitation is an ethical and strategic way of getting the message out to as many different groups as possible.

5. Website

As websites have become an information highway for everything in the district, the very same absolutely holds true for the referendum. A tab or page should be established to post all information about the projects, a needs assessment identifying the projects that have been identified for repair or construction, and the potential tax impact associated with the costs of the referendum. This part of the site should also include any presentations that have been given (for those individuals to view who were unable to attend sessions) and literature that has provided for the referendum projects that were made available to all stakeholder groups.

6. E-mail for Questions and Answers

A special e-mail address or account can be created to allow the superintendent or a designee accept questions and provide answers in consideration of the referendum projects, items associated with projects, concerns with the process or information, and campaign ideas or just to "vent" in support or disdain for your proposal. The address will most likely be an easy reference to the project (e.g., referendum@anydistrict.org; referendum_questions@ eaglerockschools.edu) and the address should be posted in multiple places and in school newsletters.

7. Multiple Languages

In order to ensure a completely transparent process and inform as many potential voters as possible about the upcoming election, a superintendent will consider translating all informational pieces into the top two most spoken languages in the district other than English. Another consideration may be to inform native speakers, through literature, that Spanish-, Polish-, and other language–speaking staff members are available to answer questions.

8. Host Building Tours

Parents and community members must be invited to tour building sites and witness the needed repairs for themselves. Hosting tours of buildings with the district architect of record and/or the director of buildings and grounds can provide evidence that your assessment is viable and was prepared with due diligence. A superintendent should ensure to host these tours after school hours, weekends, or other days when schools are not in session.

SUMMARY AND FUTURE CONSIDERATIONS

Passing a referendum construction project can be one of the most important duties that a superintendent has during his tenure in district. Maintaining and repairing physical structures is a major safety consideration along with building new schools and additions due to enrollment and programmatic concerns. A superintendent must be involved in every step of the referendum process as well as the construction once an affirmative vote is attained. Taxpayers must feel confident that the projects set forth will benefit them, specifically when it comes to property values.

The chief administrator must establish that confidence and be extremely visible to present the importance of each project and answer the hard questions for community stakeholders. Although an arsenal of supporting personnel (consultants, architects, bond counsel, etc.) can be involved to assist the superintendent in this endeavor, nothing replaces a "grassroots" campaign led by the superintendent herself. The hard work and time spent will definitely pay off and improve the community as a whole.

In addition, consider the following:

- What obstacles will a superintendent ultimately face during a referendum campaign and subsequent vote?
- How does politics play a major role in this important process, especially considering the support of local municipal or city government and upcoming elections?

Notes

CHAPTER 1

1. Based on, Banks, James A. (2012). "Introduction." *Encyclopedia of diversity in education* (Vol. 1, xlvii–liii). Los Angeles: SAGE Reference.

CHAPTER 2

1. Reis, B. (2011). The importance of listing so-called protected classes in antibullying laws and policies. Safe Schools Coalition.
2. Stop Bullying.gov. (2014).
3. Ibid.
4. Ibid.
5. Antidiscrimination, civil rights statute that requires the needs of students with disabilities to be met as adequately as the needs of the nondisabled are met.
6. Küpper, L. (2009). Questions often asked by parents about special education services. Center for Parent Information and Resources.
7. Pub. L. No. 93–112, 87 Stat. 394 (September 26, 1973), codified at 29 U.S.C. § 701 et seq.
8. Durheim, M. (2010). A parent's guide to Section 504 in public schools. Great Kids!
9. Americans with Disabilities Act of 1990, as amended (2009).
10. *Id.* at 6.
11. Durheim, M. (2013). A parent's guide to Section 504 in public schools. Great Kids!
12. Law Digest. (2014). United States Compulsory Education Overview.
13. Ibid.
14. Ibid.
15. Ibid.

16. NJDOE. (2014). New Jersey Department of Education website.
17. Ibid.
18. Ibid.
19. Justia. (1925). *Pierce v. Society of Sisters.*
20. Ibid.
21. Homeschooling. (2014, November 27). In *Wikipedia, the Free Encyclopedia.*
22. Ibid.
23. Hammons, C. W. (2001). School@Home. *Education Next, 1*(4), 48–55.
24. U.S. Department of Education, National Center for Education Statistics. (2017).
25. Lyman, I. (1998). Homeschooling: Back to the future? Cato Policy Analysis, 294.
26. Lines, P. M. (2000). When homeschoolers go to school: A partnership between families and schools. *Peabody Journal of Education, 75,* 159–186.
27. Homeschooling. (2014).
28. Klicka, C. J. (2004). Academic statistics on homeschooling. *Home School Legal Defense Association.* Purcelville, VA.
29. Civic Impulse. (2016). S. 1177–114th Congress: Every Student Succeeds Act.
30. Byrnes, J. P. (2008). *Cognitive development and learning in instructional contexts.* Pearson Education: Boston
31. Richardson, V. (1998). How teachers change. *Focus on Basics, 2*(C), 1–10.
32. Lepine, S. A. (2007). *The ruler and the ruled: Complicating a theory of teaching autonomy* (Doctoral dissertation). Accession Order No. 3291145, UT Electronic Dissertations and Theses, Austin, TX.
33. Hoy, A.W., & Spero, R. B. (2005). Changes in teacher efficacy during the early years of teaching: A comparison of four measures. *Teaching and Teacher Education, 21*(4), 343–356.

CHAPTER 3

1. Hubner, J., & Wolfson, J. (1996). *Somebody else's children: The courts, the kids, and the struggle to save America's troubled families.* New York, NY: Crown Publishers.
2. McGuire, A. L., & Bruce, C. R. (2008). Keeping children's secrets: Confidentiality in the physician patient relationship. *Houston Journal of Health Law & Policy*, (8), 315–333, 315. ISSN 1534–7907.
3. English, A. (2010). *State minor consent laws: A summary* (3rd ed.). Chapel Hill, NC: Center for Adolescent Health & the Law.
4. Boonstra, H., & Nash, E. (2000, August). Minors and the right to consent to health care. The Guttmacher Report on Public Policy.
5. Ibid. at 1.
6. Arizona, California, Colorado, Connecticut, the District of Columbia, Florida, Georgia, Hawaii, Indiana, Iowa, Kentucky, Maryland, Michigan, Minnesota, Mississippi, Missouri, Nebraska, New Hampshire, New Jersey, New Mexico,

New York, North Carolina, North Dakota, Ohio, Oklahoma, Rhode Island, South Dakota, Texas, Utah, Vermont, Virginia, Washington, Wisconsin, and Wyoming.

7. Coleman, D. L., & Rosoff, P. M. (2013, April). The legal authority of mature minors to consent to general medical treatment. *Pediatrics, 131*(4), 786–793.
8. Ibid. at 3.
9. English, A., & Ford, C. (2004). The HIPAA privacy rule and adolescents: Legal questions and clinical challenges. *Perspectives on Sexual and Reproductive Health, 36*(2), 80–86.
10. American Civil Liberties Union NJ. (2008). Minor's access to reproductive healthcare. Physicians for Reproductive Choice and Health. http://www.prch.org
11. The HIPAA Privacy Rule (45 CFR Part 160 and Subparts A and E of Part 164) establishes national standards to protect individuals' medical records and other personal information. The rule gives patients rights over their health information, including rights to examine and obtain a copy of their health records and to request corrections.
12. Ibid. at 1.
13. FERPA is a federal law that is administered by the Family Policy Compliance Office (Office) in the U.S. Department of Education. 20 U.S.C. § 1232g; 34 CFR Part 99. FERPA applies to educational agencies and institutions (e.g., schools) that receive funding under any program administered by the department.
14. U.S. Department of Education. (2015). FERPA.
15. 1. False; 2. False; 3. False (as long as they are claimed as a dependent for Internal Revenue Service purposes); 4. False; 5. False (no specified time); 6. False; 7. True; 8. True; 9. True; 10. True.

CHAPTER 4

1. Wolf, K.C. (2013, Fall). Booking students: An analysis of school arrests and court outcomes. *Northwestern Journal of Law & Social Policy, 9*(1), 58. Article 3.
2. Fabelo, T., Thompson, M.D., Plotkin, M., Carmichael, D., Marchbanks, M.P., & Booth, E.A. (2011). Breaking schools' rules: A statewide study of how school discipline relates to students' success and juvenile justice involvement. The Council of State Governments Justice Center & Public Policy Research Institute.
3. A document providing guidelines to ensure that a local police department and school district have a shared understanding of the role and responsibilities of each in maintaining safe schools, improving school climate, and supporting educational opportunities for all students.
4. Browne, J.A. (2003). Derailed! The schoolhouse to jailhouse track. Advancement Project: Washington, D.C.

5. Robers, S., Zhang, J., Truman, J., & Snyder, T.D. (2010). Indicators of school crime and safety: 2010. National Center for Education Statistics & Bureau of Justice Statistics,, http://nces.ed.gov/pubs2011/2011002.pdf; Hirschfield, Paul J. (2008). Preparing for prison? The criminalization of school discipline in the USA. *Theoretical Criminology, 12*(1), 79–101.

6. Ibid.

7. SROs are trained police officers who are stationed in schools, most commonly through agreements between school districts and local police departments.

8. Advancement Project. Model MOU between a school district and a police or sheriff's department.

9. U.S. Department of Education. (2005). FERPA.

10. Ibid.

11. Ibid.

12. Ibid. at 1.

13. A proactive approach to establishing the behavioral supports and social culture is needed for all students in a school to achieve social, emotional, and academic success. Attention is focused on sustaining primary, secondary, and individual systems of support that improve the lifestyle (e.g., personal, health, social, family, work, recreation) of an individual by making misbehavior less relevant and desired behavior more functional or rewarding.

14. Ibid. at 1.

15. Ibid. at 4.

16. Nolan, K. (2012). *Police in the hallways: Discipline in an urban high school.* University of Minnesota Press: Minneapolis; Kupchik, A. (2009). Things are tough all over: Race, ethnicity, class and school discipline. *Punishment & Society, 11*(3), 291, 299.

17. Devine, J. (1996). *Maximum security: The culture of violence in inner city schools.* Chicago University Press: Chicago, IL.

18. April 20, 1999.

19. Ibid. at 16 (Kupchik); Lyons, W., & Drew, J. (2006). *Punishing schools: Fear and citizenship in American public schools* (pp. 44–46). The University of Michigan Press: Ann Arbor.

20. Dohrn, B. (2001). (Citing Dorfman, L., and Schiraldi, V. (2001). Off-Balance: Youth, race and crime in the news. Building Blocks for Youth. Youth Law Center, Washington, D.C.).

21. Ibid. at 9.

22. Ibid. at 2.

23. Fein, R.A., Vossekuil, B., Pollack, W.S., Borum, R., Modzeleski, W., & Reddy, M. (2002). Threat assessment in schools: A guide to managing threatening situations and to creating safe school climates. Washington, D.C.

24. Cornell, D. G. (2012). Guidelines for responding to student threats of violence: Virginia Youth Violence Project. Curry School of Education, University of Virginia. Student threat assessment as a violence prevention strategy, presentation July 17, 2012, Workshop Aggression, Luxembourg City, Luxembourg.

25. Ibid.

26. Ibid.

27. Ibid.
28. Center for Behavioral Health Statistics and Quality. (2016). Key substance use and mental health indicators in the United States: Results from the 2015 National Survey on Drug Use and Health (HHS Publication No. SMA 16–4984, NSDUH Series H-51). Retrieved from http://www.samhsa.gov/data/
29. Definition from New Jersey Department of Education.
30. As defined in most policy manuals of public school districts.
31. http://www.state.nj.us/education/students/safety/behavior/hib/
32. Ibid.

CHAPTER 5

1. *Griego v. Hogan*, 377 P.2d 953, 955–56 (N.M. 1963).
2. Blokhuis, J. C. (2012). Public educational authority and children's rights from a *parens patriae* perspective. Social Development Studies Round Table Series, Waterloo University.
3. Homeless Assistance Act of 1987 (Pub. L. 100–77, July 22, 1987, 101 Stat. 482, 42 U.S.C. § 11301 et seq.).
4. Ibid.
5. Education for Homeless Children and Youth Program. (2004). McKinney-Vento Homeless Education Assistance Improvements Act of 2001. Part C. Subtitle B. Section 721.
6. Ibid.

CHAPTER 6

1. Lafee, S. (2013, August). The schools' role in students' mental health. *School Administrator, 7*(70), 24–30.
2. National Institutes of Health (U.S.). (2007). Biological Sciences Curriculum Study. Bethesda, MD: National Institutes of Health.
3. Satcher, D. (2000, February). *Mental health: A report of the surgeon general—executive summary. Professional Psychology: Research and Practice, 31*(1), 5–13.
4. Mental Health: A report of the surgeon general. (1999). U.S. Public Health Service. National Institute of Mental Health.
5. Adelman, H., & Taylor, L. (Directors). School Mental Health Project, Dept. of Psychology, UCLA, Los Angeles, CA 90095–1563.
6. Ibid.
7. Teenmentalhealth.org. Accessed January 1, 2016. http://www.teenmentalhealth.org
8. Sifferlin, A. (2014, October 7). Why schools should screen their students' mental health. *Time*.

9. Ibid. at 1.
10. Los Angeles Unified SD. Mental Health.
11. Ibid. at 1.
12. Ibid. at 1.
13. Ibid. at 1.

CHAPTER 7

1. Centers for Disease Control and Prevention. (2013). *Voluntary guidelines for managing food allergies in schools and early care and education programs.* Washington, DC: U.S. Department of Health and Human Services.
2. CDC. (1999). *Impact of vaccines universally recommended for children–United States, 1900–1998.* JAMA. 281, 1482–1483.
3. Shefer, A., Briss, P.A., Rodewald, L. Bernier, R., Strikas, R., Yusuf, H., Ndiaye, S., Williams, S., Pappaioanou, M., & Hinman, A. R. (1999). Improving immunization coverage rates: An evidence-based review of the literature. *Epidemiologic Reviews, 21*(1), 96, 124–127.
4. Referring to those individuals who oppose population-based vaccination requirements.
5. Hodge, J. G., Jr., & Gostin, L. O. (2001). School vaccination requirements: Historical, social, and legal perspectives. *Kentucky Law Journal, 90*(4), 831.
6. Hazen v. Strong, 2 Vt. 417 (1830).
7. Briss, P.A., Rodewald, L.E., Hinman, A.R., Shefer, A.M., Strikas, R.A., Bernier, R.R., Carande-Kulis, V.G., Yusuf, H.R., Ndiaye, S.M., & Williams, S.M. (2000). Reviews of evidence regarding interventions to improve vaccination coverage in children, adolescents, and adults. *American Journal of Preventive Medicine, 18*, 97, 104.
8. Flanders, G. (2000). Vaccinations: Public health's miracle under scrutiny, state legislatures, *26*(3), 20.
9. CDC school vaccination information can be found at https://www.cdc.gov/phlp/docs/school-vaccinations.pdf
10. Condition or factor that serves as a reason to withhold a certain medical treatment due to the harm that it would cause the patient.

CHAPTER 10

1. Asbestos Hazard Emergency Response Act (AHERA).

About the Author

Richard D. Tomko, PhD, has had numerous administrative responsibilities during his twenty-year career in educational administration. He has been a building administrator at the middle and secondary levels and responsible for district-wide curriculum, assessment, innovative program initiatives, technology, and professional development while in central office positions. Tomko has dedicated his career to serving communities as an educational leader, acting as a director, assistant principal, principal, assistant superintendent, and superintendent in both private and public school systems. He earned a Doctor of Philosophy degree in Educational Leadership, Management, and Policy from Seton Hall University; earned a Master of Jurisprudence from Loyola University Chicago School of Law; and holds certificates in Community and Economic Development from the Pennsylvania State University, and the Brain, Mind, and Teaching from Johns Hopkins University. He is an adjunct professor at several universities and works as a consultant to educational institutions and families.

Tomko and his wife, Jaimie, cofounded WISPER (We Invest in Strong Programs, Empowerment, and Building Respect for Women), a 501(c)3 organization established to assist and recognize individuals and their mentors who deserve support in helping to fulfill the mission of "Paying It Forward" by leveling the proverbial playing field in the spirit of equality for all through the advancement of leadership, nurturing of future career paths, representing community ideals, and enhancing academic standards in education.

Tomko is a change agent for creativity and problem solving and works with administrative teams to decrease achievement gaps between demographic subgroups of learners by involving families, stakeholders, and community groups in the restoration of student engagement leading to overall student success.